CW01329508

The Architectural Sketches of Henning Larsen

Published with generous support from

Bestles Fond
Henning Larsens Fond

K: Danish Arts Foundation

Merete Ahnfeldt-Mollerup

The Architectural Sketches of **Henning Larsen**

Strandberg Publishing

7	Preface
9	Drawing architecture
23	Studies 1948-1951
39	Youth
45	The beginning of the office
71	Mother Denmark
77	Three projects in conversation
93	MoFA
133	Copenhagen Business School and Dalgas Have
143	Sketchbook from Malta

Sketch, MoFA

Preface

The drawings presented here are a small selection taken from the many thousands left by Henning Larsen. He drew throughout life and repeatedly stated that he saw the professional use of sketches as the most important tool of an architect.

The many different sketches in the complete collection both demonstrate the many tasks of the architect, from the conceptual sketch to the final project details, and show a life's development, from the young student to the head of a large office.

This selection strives to show the breadth as well as the development of the collection.

As a parameter, all the project sketches are chosen from just before Henning Larsen began at architecture school in 1949 and the period up to and including 1985, during which time the projects for the Business School and Dalgas Have were designed and when the Ministry of Foreign Affairs in Riyadh was completed. At this time, Henning Larsen Architects became one of the first architecture offices in Denmark to introduce CAD (computer-aided design). This didn't mean that Henning Larsen or the other architects in the office stopped drawing by hand, but it gradually changed the role of freehand drawing in a manner that is too large a subject for this small book.

Today there is a growing international interest in freehand sketching among architects and, at the same time, a wider discussion of the photorealist visualizations used by architects and planners. As a young man, Henning Larsen rebelled against the visualizations of that age, creating carefully made, beautiful watercolour paintings that took days to produce. Perhaps today these drawings can contribute to the discussion of how hand sketching contributes to the quality of architecture.

At the end of the book are some sketches from later in Henning Larsen's life, when he often holidayed on Malta. Here one can see how the hand-drawn sketch as a visual, analytical tool went everywhere with him, even on holiday, and how his field of interest was not limited to architecture and planning but included the other visual arts, in all their forms.

Thank you to the Bestles Fond, Henning Larsens Fond and Danish Arts Foundation for its support (insert other foundations here with help from Strandberg, I have lost count) and to the Danish Art Library for the kind help during many hours of research.

Merete Ahnfeldt-Mollerup
September, 2022

Drawing architecture

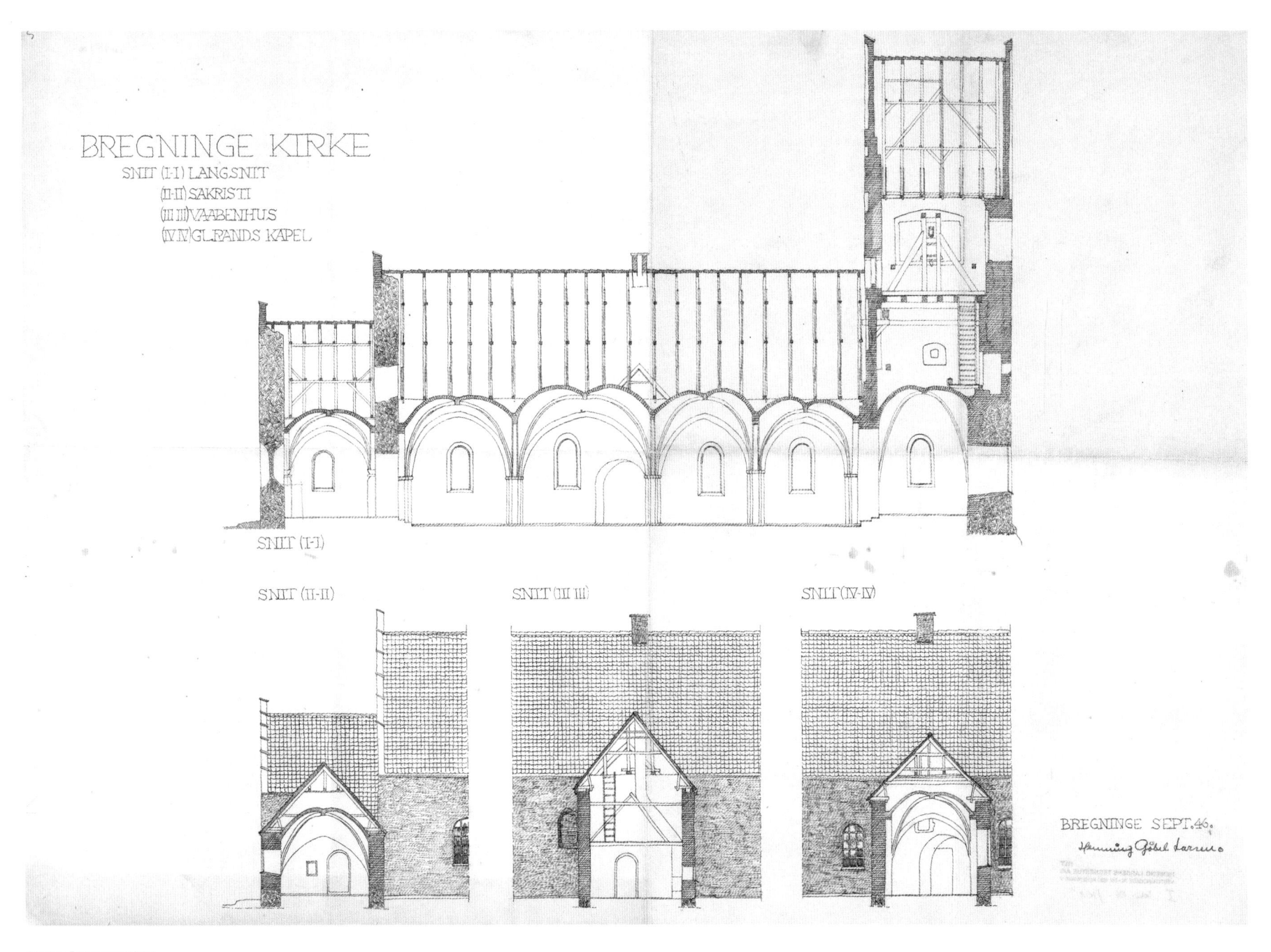

Survey, Bregninge Kirke

For most architects, drawings are the most important design tool. Today, designers make use of different computer programs, but throughout time their methods and tools have changed, depending on what was available and possible. Even though contemporary computer programs work with three-dimensional virtual models, they still refer to projection drawings: from your mental or computer model, you can draw horizontal and vertical sections, as if you were slicing it with a knife. Vertical slices are called sections; horizontal slices are plans. A facade is technically a section drawn in front of the structure. Hand-drawn sections are made to scale and are dimensionally stable. On the computer the whole model is in full scale, and it is when you extract a section that you choose a scale to see on the screen or in print.

When all architectural drafting was done by hand, before the mid 1990s, all countries would have a fixed set of scales that were commonly used. In Denmark, those were the metric scales of 1:1000, 1:500, 1:200, 1:100, 1:50, 1:20, 1:5 and 1:1. Sometimes furniture designers would use 1:10. The repetitive use of fixed scales meant that the architect could draw 'to measure' in freehand, which is often seen in Henning Larsen's sketches.

When using this method, one cannot see everything in every drawing, and because of that there is a natural hierarchy of knowledge in the design process, where each jump in scale introduces new questions and answers. In today's frequently used object-based digital modelling, you need to determine the actual window in order to use a window in your design. In the hand sketch, you can just indicate a window and then wait until it becomes relevant to determine the properties of that window. It is advantageous that you don't have to deal with too much information early on in the process but can resolve the different problems in turn.

A project for a building or an installation comprises a whole set of drawings and models in different scales. Together, the drawings and models contain a very large amount of data, information and knowledge in a systematic and hierarchic order. In principal, the competent practitioner can read this set of drawings as a spatial whole, just like some musicians can 'hear' a whole symphony in their head when they read the sheet music, though it is very hard. The Danish architect Mogens Lassen spoke of having a 'perfect spatial pitch', an ability as rare among architects as perfect pitch is among musicians. Even for an architect with such a perfect spatial pitch, the projects must still been drawn. There is no need for a perfect finished form in the mind to be illustrated; there may be just a vague thought or even a diagram or a principle. There is a method for the development of projects, and this method is clearly visible in the sketches of Henning Larsen.

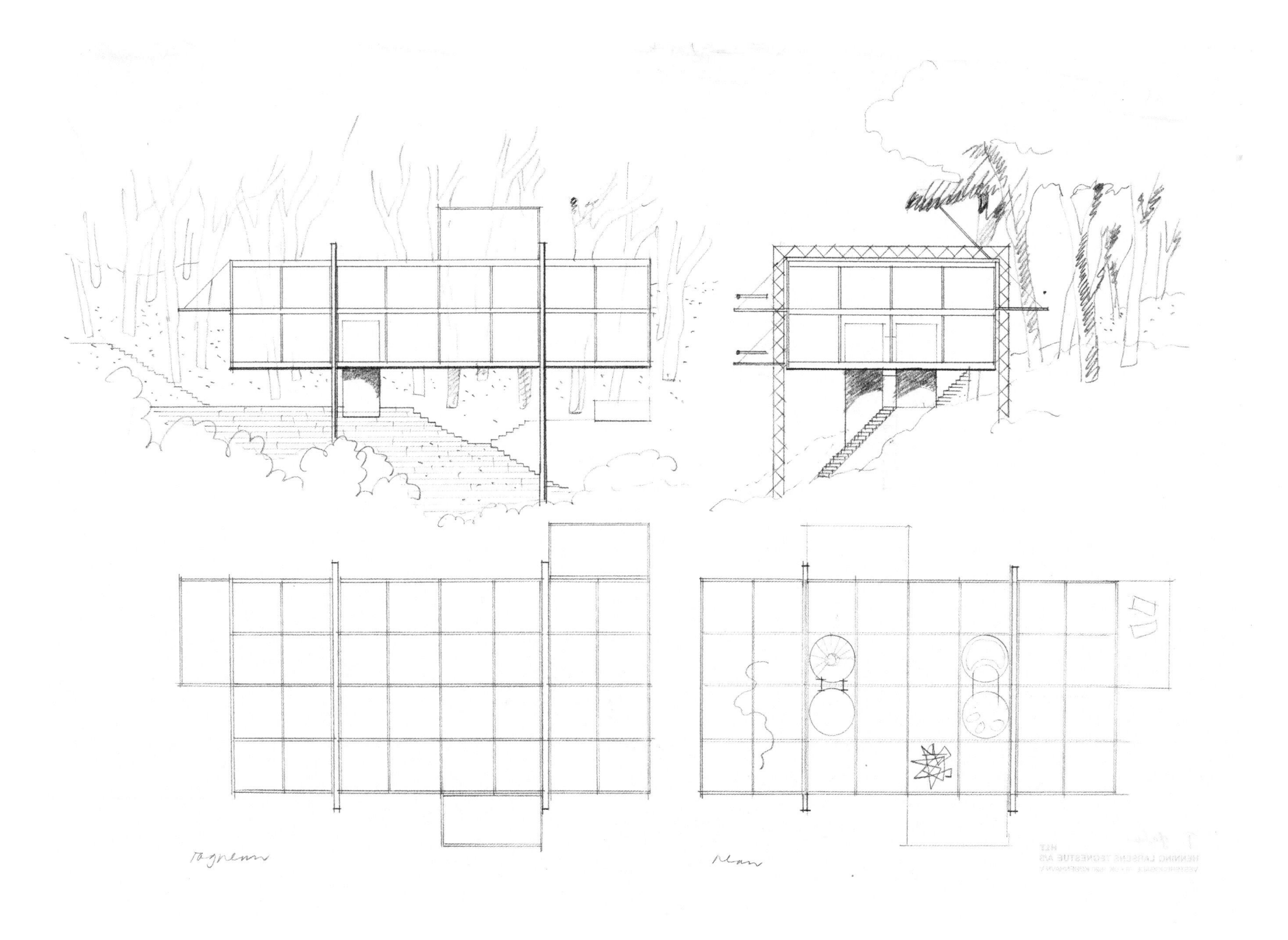

School project, glass house

Drawing architecture

The modern approach to sketching with projection drawings was developed during the late Middle Ages and the Renaissance, on the basis of previous, more diagrammatic drawings. Over time, there was a gradual development of the paper and of the tools for drawing – the ruler, the triangle and the compass – tools that mirrored the measuring tools on site. As Henning Larsen wrote in lecture notes during the 1990s:

> *When you draw with your hand on a piece of paper, in a way you are miming the reality of the site. During sketching, the hand and pencil are slowly repeating, almost crafting, the processes that later will happen in reality, when the elements and materials are produced in the shops and on site, etc.*

Sketch,
opera in Paris

When Henning Larsen was a student at the Royal Academy of Fine Arts in Copenhagen, around 1950, architects worked very much the same way as a hundred years before. The development of cheap tracing paper had meant that the role of geometry had changed during the nineteenth century. Where before, it had been necessary to construct the drawings so they could be reproduced without too much effort, now tracing paper made it possible to simply add a new layer to make reproductions or changes. The compliance of many different plans and sections became easier to handle, too: by laying tracing paper over a plan, you could 'raise' the sections and facades in the correct measurements without the painstaking work of geometric construction.

At the Royal Academy of Fine Arts during the late 1940s and early 1950s, great emphasis was put on the harmony of form and construction. The form of a building had to fit with brick measurements and the timber lengths used in the floors, which were shown as dashed lines on the plans. With modular concrete construction, the beams were replaced by dashed lines showing the main modular system. As a consequence, all buildings were defined by an underlying common order known by all the different professions within the construction industry, including architects, engineers and builders. Even in apparently free-form sketches, that order would be present and recognizable to professionals.

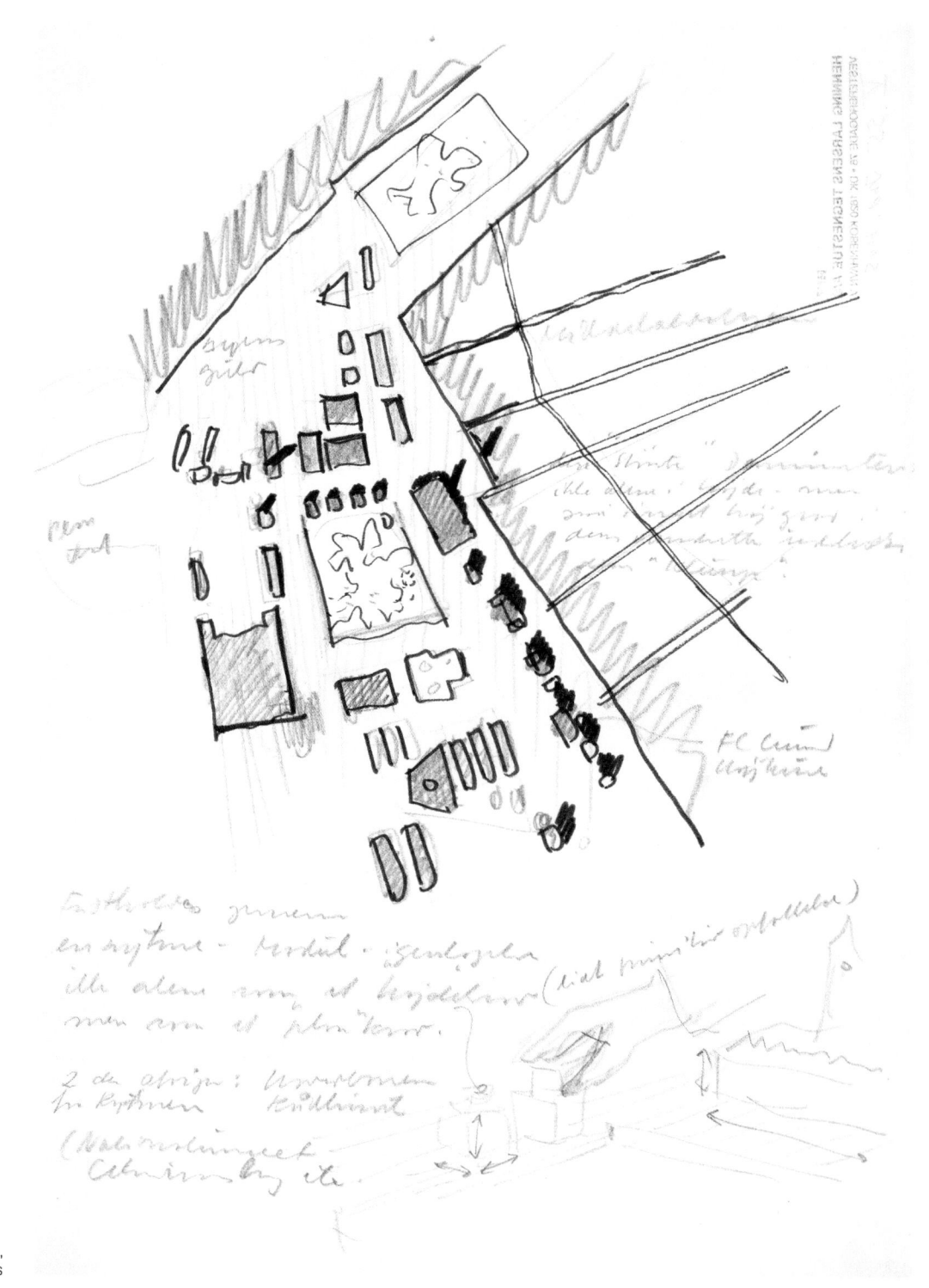

Sketch, Industriens Hus

Today, most architects and engineers only use their pens and paper for freehand sketches, like those in this book. They do this when they are sitting together in teams and solving problems of any scale within a given task, with the drawings as part of the dialogue process. Many still use sketching as part of their personal reflections on a project, but with the arrival of computer-aided design, freehand sketches changed. Skills like drawing to scale and thinking about the order of the building simultaneously with the form are rare today, because they are no longer necessary. And that again subtly changes the shapes of the buildings that are actually built.

The first measured, constructed drawings for a project are the site plan and sections, often in a very large scale. The architect can place tracing paper over a map of the site and redraw the map, emphasizing aspects they find interesting and leaving out less-relevant information. Here, the drawing examines the plan. With Henning Larsen, these initial explorations were instantly followed by sections and spatial sketches in the same scale. There might already be an idea, a principle to explore, but more often there were many experiments during this phase, attempts that can sometimes hardly be recognized as buildings or space but are more like geometric diagrams, indicating the main order.

Even if many of these initial sketches are on random pieces of paper, they are generally drawn to scale. The measurements and proportions are then in the hand and mind of the architect after the initial explorations of the site map.

Maybe it would be meaningful to try out several of the diagrams in a more detailed scale. Maybe several architects in the office would develop different schemes. Larsen went from table to table, often commenting with drawings rather than words.

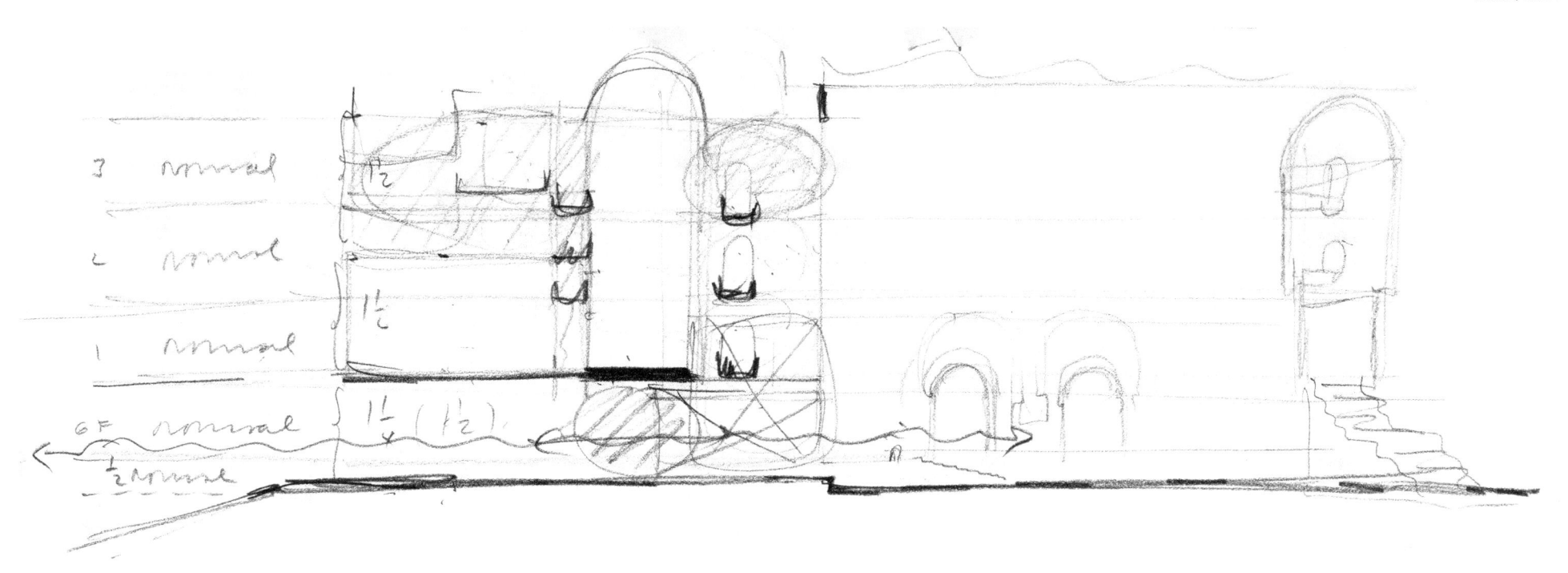

Sketch, MoFA

It is a principle of architectural method that one begins with the bigger context in 'small' drawings and then moves closer in with ever 'larger' drawings, for instance from 1:1000 to 1:20. But even though the main process is from a large scale towards a small one, any new step may uncover a detail that leads to changes in the whole, or the other way round. Perhaps the standard module has to be changed in the middle of the process, or there is a development in the relation between the technical section of the facade in 1:20 and the whole length of the facade in 1:100.

Both the accurately drafted projection drawings and the freehand sketches by Henning Larsen are limited to the most important information. This is a clear break with the Danish tradition which was forcefully upheld by the professor, dean and editor Kay Fisker. Kay Fisker was from a young age a very important figure in the development of Danish architecture in the twentieth century, and he was critical towards modern architecture, though not a historicist like the generation before him. He imagined a modern vernacular architecture, based on local materials and crafts, primarily brick. For him, the survey of historical buildings was an important source of knowledge about design, and the detailed form of drawing which is necessary in that context informed the style of drawing he preferred when designing new buildings. His influence can still be seen today, in the built works of Danish architects and in the teaching at the Royal Academy School of Architecture.

The focus on materiality in the drawings leads naturally to a focus on materiality in the actual building, often with beautiful sensually formed buildings as a result. But in some cases it can lead to a lack of interest in the spatial manifestation of the building in favour of the materiality of the facade.

It was in this context that Larsen, already as a young man, found inspiration in Le Corbusier's very simple line drawings, which featured little or no indications of materials, except in the actual detail drawings, and allowed him to keep a sharp focus on space and spatial sequences and what these would imply.

While developing a project on paper and in physical models, it is very important to maintain an overview of the whole project and all its parts. With large projects consisting of many employees working on different parts, it is also important that everyone knows the same information. There isn't one drawing or model that defines the project but rather relations between all the drawings and models. There are plans, sections and facades in different scales, and they need to be seen together in a meaningful order, beginning with the site plan, where one sees the project in its context, and ending with important details. Spatial depictions and models are applied where they are relevant. Henning Larsen often made little 'presentation plans', for himself or as part of a discussion, where he sketched which drawings he found necessary for the development and description of the project.

Another aspect of the project management of great post-war architecture was the relation between modular planning and simple geometries. Especially after 1960, the scale and programmatic complexity of hospitals, universities, office buildings, cultural institutions and even housing was unprecedented and defined the careers of Henning Larsen and many of his peers, nationally and internationally. The methods used in pre-war design were not all suitable for these new tasks. The challenge was to maintain spatial, architectonic quality in these large projects without losing the whole. The order from the construction site became an important guideline for the projects, which comprised many thousands of square metres, as did the geometries that reflected both the drafting tools and the machinery on site.

Nearly all of the drawings for the Foreign Ministry in Riyadh – many hundreds of drawings – were drawn using a parallel straight edge, a 45° drafting triangle and a compass. That way, the development of the project remained a rational process that led to a rational construction process, with no loss of poetry in the final result, in spite of the rigid method.

When a project takes shape, it is essential for the quality of the final structure that the architects can evaluate the drawings analytically and critically. This can happen in a direct manner, by correcting drawings, which are then redrawn; the consequences of these are then added to all the other drawings. But Henning Larsen had a habit or practice of sketching important aspects of a project again and again, often with almost no alterations. It is obvious that here he was thinking critically on the paper with his hand, and not in his head.

After the intense period of economic growth during the 1950s and 1960s, the 1970s brought a significant crisis in both fuel and the economy. At the Henning Larsen office, things weren't too bad, due to the large university projects in Trondheim and Berlin. But all over the world, the slowdown led architects to reflect on the profession, and many returned to the academic drawing practice from before modernism. When the French king established the art academies, one aspect of education for both architects and fine artists was a stipend for a stay at the French academy in Rome, the Villa Medici. Here, architects studied both classical and modern architecture by surveying and drawing. Over time, it became a tradition to make huge reconstruction drawings of classical buildings, using watercolours for extra impact. These fantasies of a lost empire became the foundation of the academic style of architectural drawing all over the world.

Even as the reconstruction drawings disappeared after the First World War, the tradition of the Prix de Rome continued, not least in the USA, where architects such as Louis Kahn and Robert Venturi found life-defining inspiration during their stays, and in particular a joy in the speculative drawing, which changed their understanding of what was possible in architecture. Over a few years, the architectural drawing found a renaissance, in a showdown with what was seen especially in the Anglo Saxon world as the monotony of modernist architecture.

During the work with Trondheim University, Larsen began to include the work with drawings, as an independent element of the project work, on a more serious level. He specifically worked with how framing is in itself an artistic choice, and with colour in strong blocks. First he was most probably inspired by the travel sketches of Louis Kahn; later there is clear inspiration from the artist David Hockney. Henning Larsen had always been curious about drawing as an art form, and all the way back to his student days there are examples of drawings that are playful and experimental, and not necessarily about architecture. He was clearly interested in graphic art; among other examples, he studied a Danish cartoonist, Axel Nygaard, and the artist Palle Nielsen. There are sketches for the chapel and crematorium in Aarhus, from 1967, where one can already find the merging of a fine-art approach and the architectural drawing more characteristic of the 1970s and onward.

Internationally, the confrontation with modernism culminated with the opening of the first Architecture Biennale in Venice in 1980, titled *Presence of the Past*. There, several of the most famous architects of the day built their speculative drawings as full-scale facades on the Strada Novissima in the Arsenale building, and Aldo Rossi built the floating Teatro del Mundo, moored at the Punta della Dogana. Henning Larsen was in Venice for the opening, which took place during the work on the Foreign Ministry in Saudi Arabia, and in his notes one finds both an analysis of the layered spaces of the Doge Palace and a sketch made with a ruler and triangle, in which he translates the knowledge from the analysis into a detail in the Ministry while also including graphic inspiration from Rossi, see p. 117.

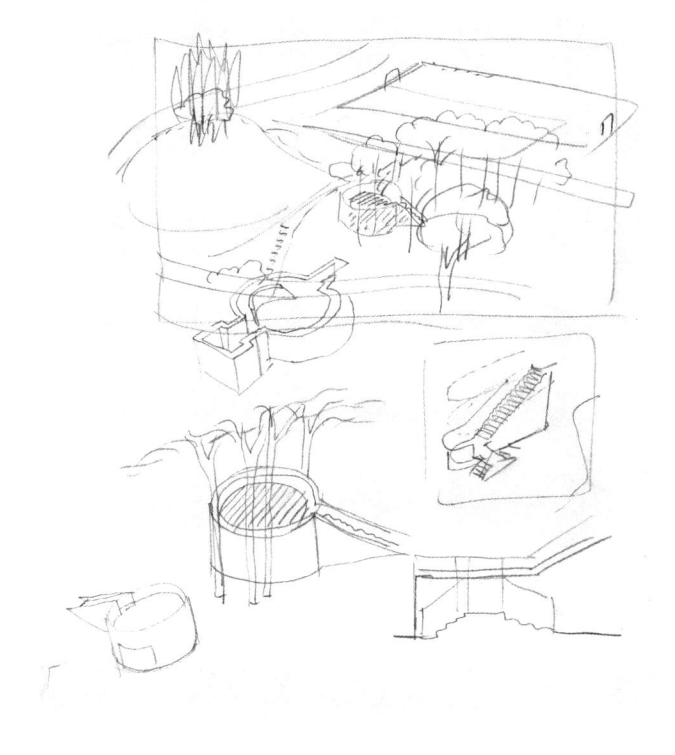

Sketch, Høje-Taastrup Amtsgymnasium

The analytical drawing – often based on a survey – plays an important part in the architectural design process. While this type of drawing requires precision, the point of the analytical drawing is not the photographic representation of an object but the examination of that object, often with a specific purpose. It can be used to understand the object's geometry, or the hierarchy of spaces or forms. Henning Larsen's analytical drawings were the precondition for his creative work, from his student days into his old age. They range from a plan or a map of a landscape to a section in a building, or an observation of people walking. For any architect, the most important ability is to see. With his drawings, Henning Larsen saw curiously and intelligently, more than what can be seen with the naked eye.

Analytical drawing,
Heri es Soani

In a lecture for the students at the Royal Academy School of Architecture, he says of the observational drawing:

> *The architect who is studying within his field will have to take a different course [from the pretty watercolour]. What counts when one is drawing an architectural reality is the attempt to understand the idea behind what one sees. One must decompose or deconstruct the architectural reality, to understand how the actual idea has been manifested, in materials, forms, spaces, planes, lines, points etc. Accordingly, how it, from being an idea, a thought, a feeling, a sensation, has become a specific physical palpable reality.*

Sketch, Chapel in Aarhus

Drawing architecture 20

Three experimental sketches

Studies
1948-1951

Sketch, Denmark

Henning Larsen entered the Royal Academy School of Architecture through the 'trade route'; back then it was possible for masons and other craftsmen to enter the school directly in the third year, the so-called Main School, because it was assumed that they had learnt both to draw and the basics of construction at trade school. From the very beginning, Larsen was inspired by the international currents, and already in his first year he was using drawing in a different way from most of his peers. Sometimes, however, he had to live up to the prevailing conventions. The professors Mogens Koch (known for his furniture) and Steen Eiler Rasmussen (known for his writings) used Charlottenborg Palace for their classes on building terminology, materials, and scale, proportion and proportionality. At the time, the school was housed in this baroque palace as well as some side buildings, and generations of Danish architects learnt from the building itself. Larsen dutifully took notes and measured details, but he also made dreamy sketches that seem inspired by Axel Nygaard.

School assignment, Charlottenborg

Free sketch, Charlottenborg

Studies 1948-1951

Experimental sketch

Drawing, house for an art collector

Studies 1948-1951

The sketches p. 28-31 from architecture school seem to be from a typical assignment: 'House for an art collector'. The project is heavily inspired by the architecture of Mies van der Rohe, but the choice of artworks, including a poetry curtain, and the idea that the artworks can be moved about are personal.

you want a bath - you can have it in the green nature you can stay in the water - only looking for the birds and the clouds - and dream - or you can take some things with you and look at them.

Drawing,
house for an art collector

Drawing,
house for an art collector

Studies 1948-1951

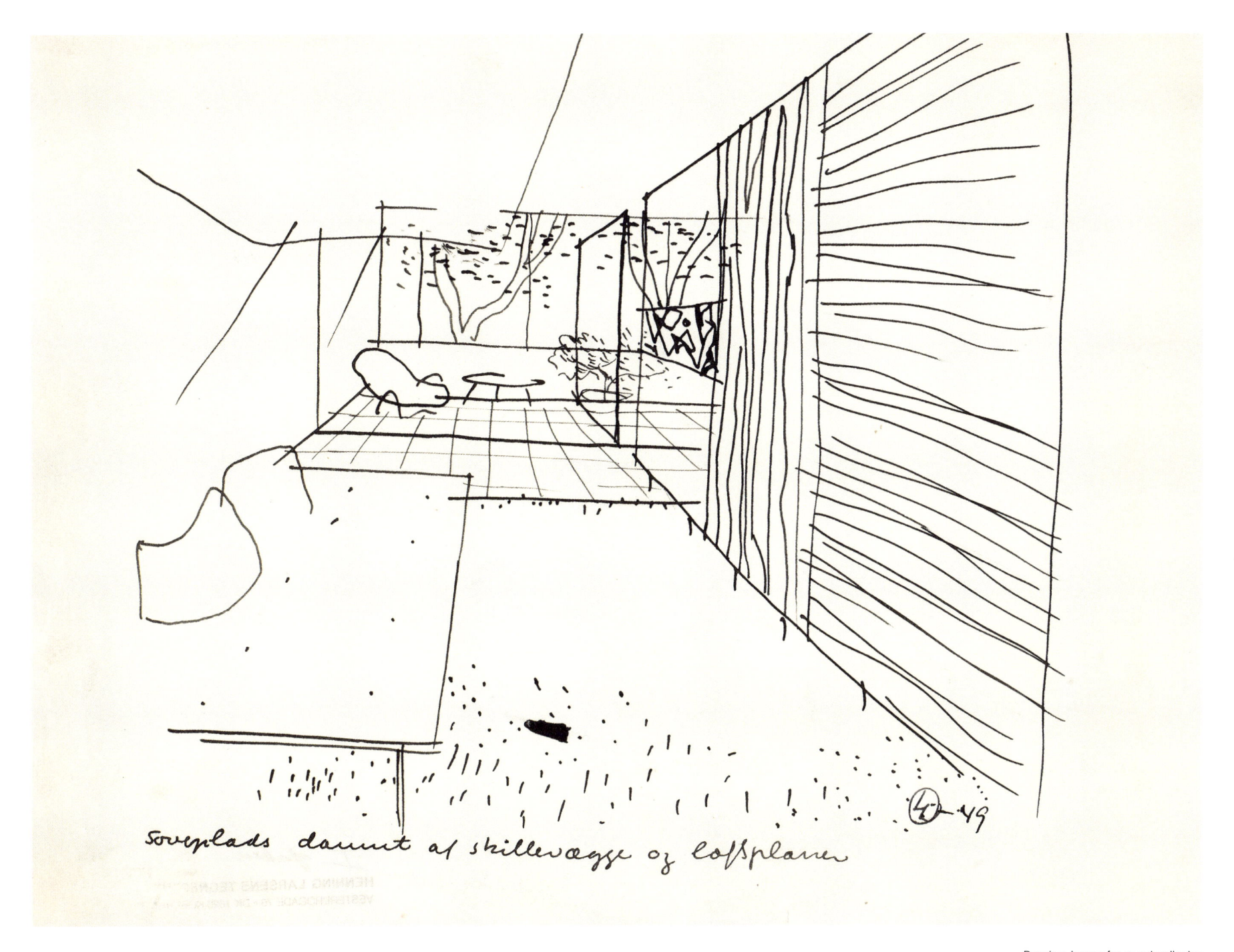

soveplads dannet af skillevægge og loftsplaner

Drawing, house for an art collector

School assignment, tall building

The first-year main assignment was for a tall building for housing. Henning Larsen was allowed to make a concrete-based design because of his trade background, but he failed spectacularly. He had to make a new, more conventional design and presentation during the holidays in order to move on to the second year of the Main School.

    In spite of the failure, there was wide recognition that Larsen was a special talent, and he was given the opportunity to go to the AA School in London as an exchange student.

School assignment, Festival of Britain

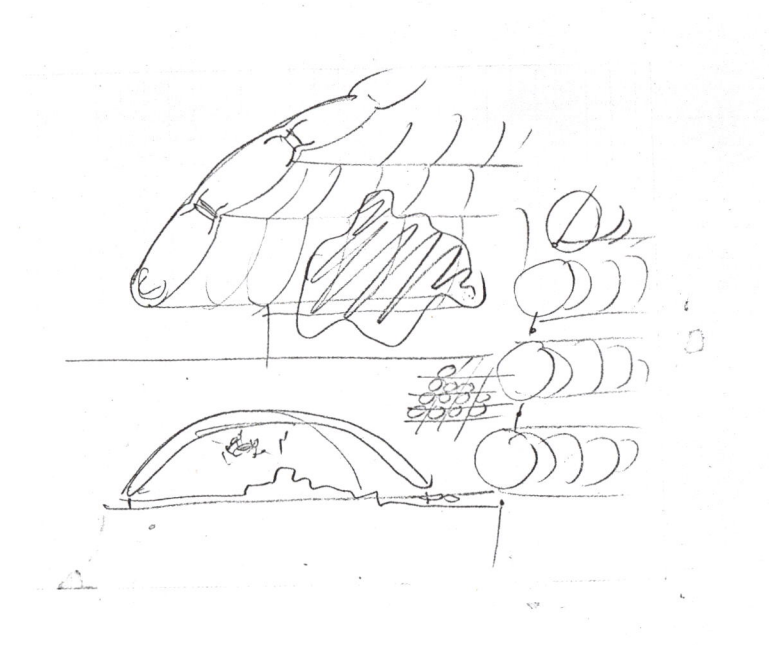

Studies 1948–1951

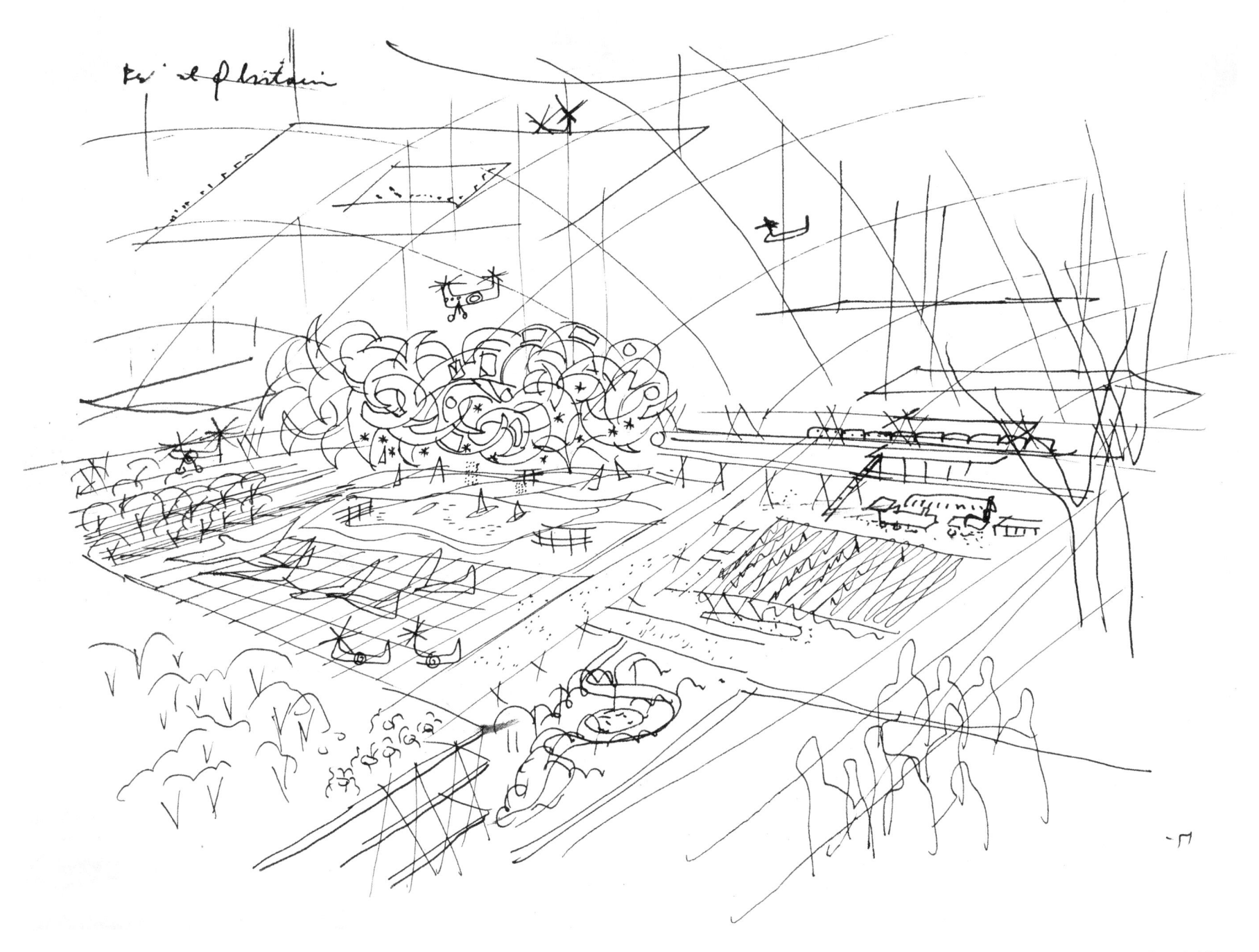

School assignment, Festival of Britain

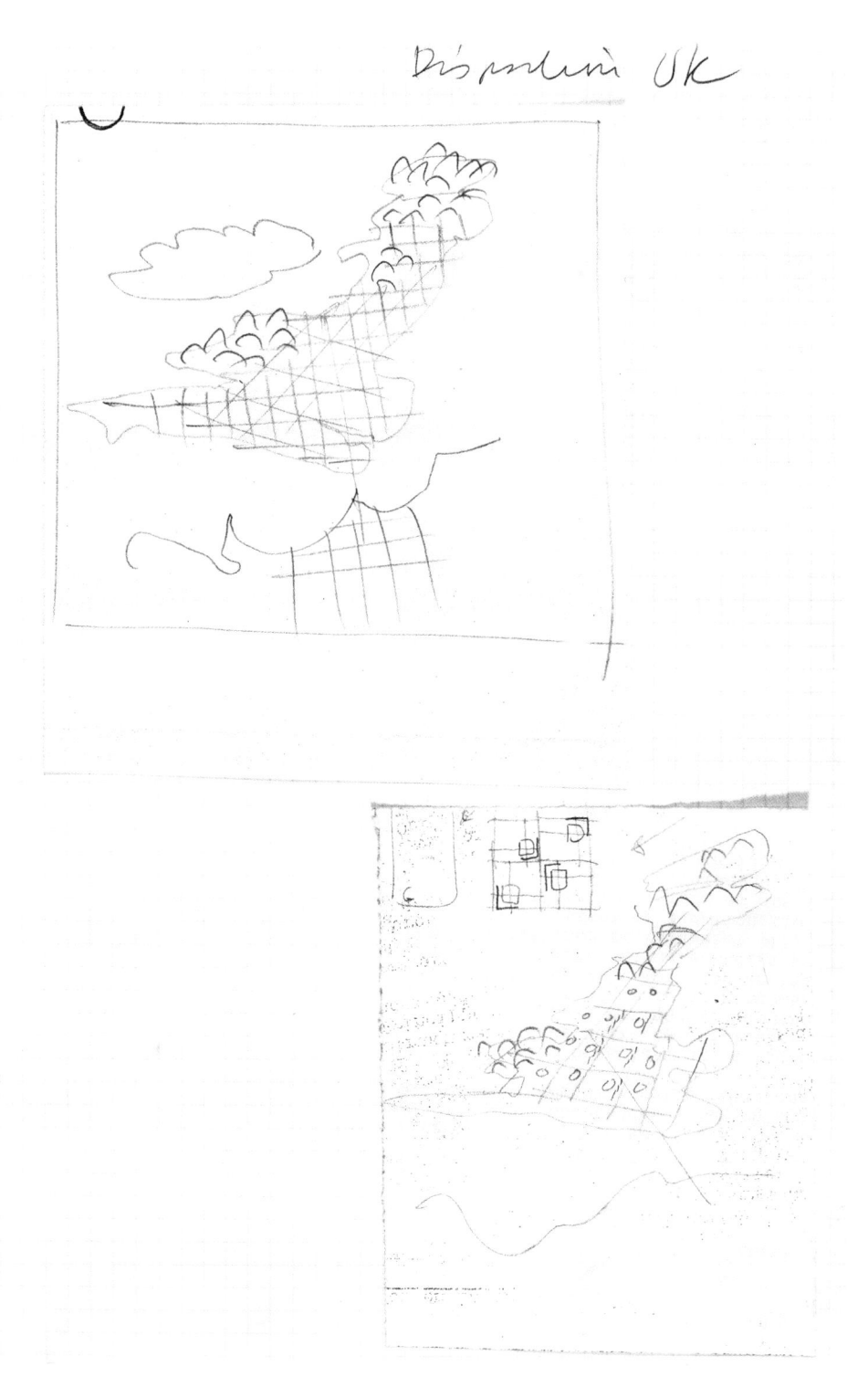

In England, one of his advisors was Arthur Korn, a member of the MARS group, a sort of think tank for architecture and planning. Korn was the *primum mobile* behind 'The MARS Plan for London', published in 1942. The plan wasn't realized in London, but it became a significant inspiration for the Copenhagen Finger Plan. Under Korn, Henning Larsen worked on a plan for all of the UK, and on a pneumatic arena for the Festival of Britain.

While the architectural education in Copenhagen was structured as mimicry of the project work in practice and was heavily focused on buildings as objects in well-defined contexts, the school in London was more preoccupied with developing processes that could help identify and solve the issues of the day. In this environment, drawing was an analytical tool with which the architect could find the relevant structures and relations for planning in large scale and for industrial construction, and also a tool with which one could define a hierarchy of scales and levels in the projects. Diagrams are important, but they are diagrams which are anchored in the specific; the mountains are where they are, as are rivers and cities. This methodology could be applied to everything, from big regional plans to teaspoons.

School assignment, large scale planning

Studies 1948-1951

School assignment, large scale planning

School assignment, large scale planning

the yard

Studies 1948-1951

Three playfull sketches

Youth

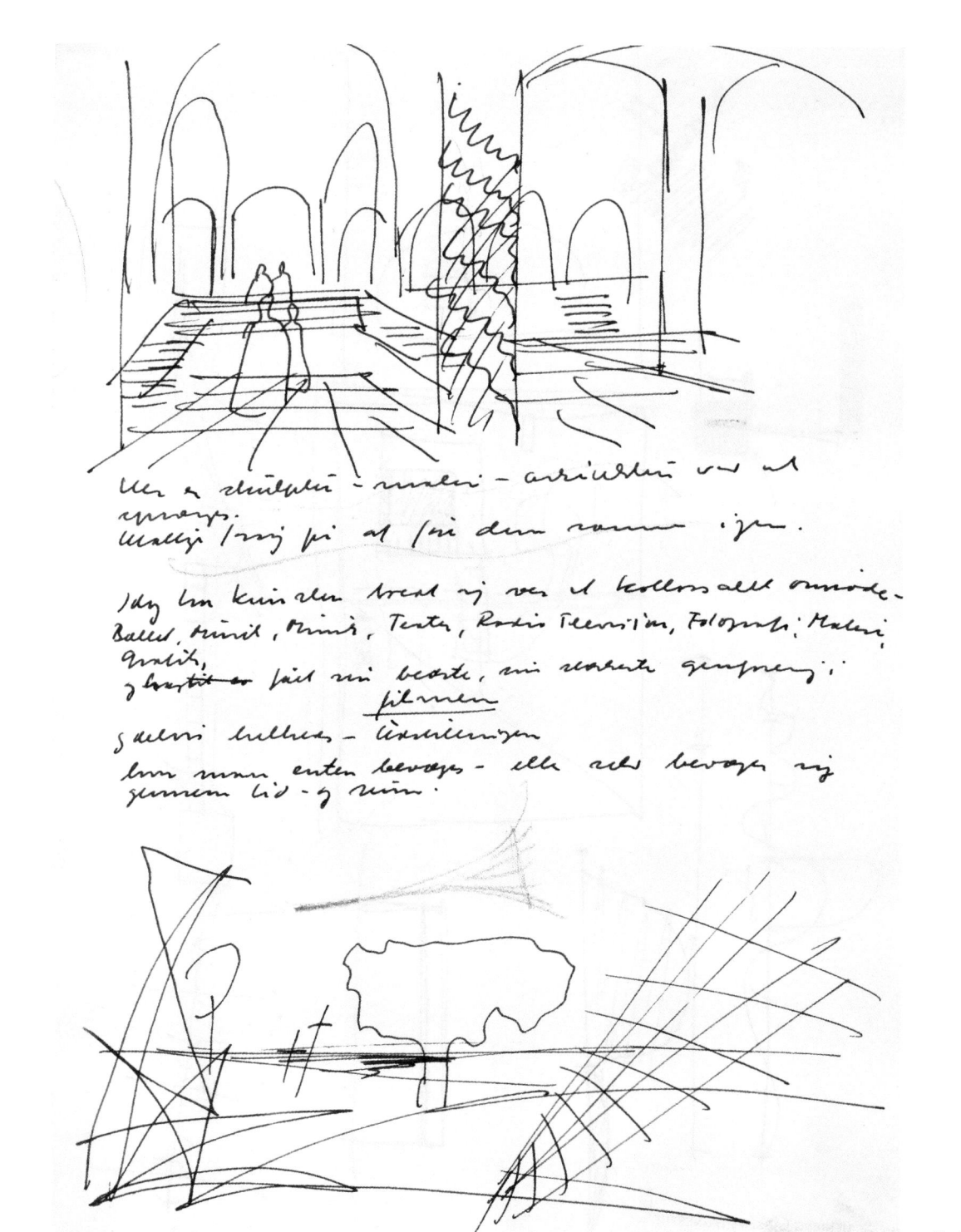

After his studies, Henning Larsen spent some years at different practices and in the newly established State Building Research Institute, which was created to support the industrialization of the construction sector, but in his spare time, he kept drawing for his own sake.

Some architectural fantasies of the type he drew during his student days can be found in the sketches for the Gold Medal competition of 1955–56, the theme of which was a building for Danish contemporary art at the Town Hall Square in Copenhagen. Again, the sketches are analytical and explorative, and of a very fundamental nature, although they are clearly inspired by the Mies van der Rohe sketches for a 'Museum for a Small City' from 1941–43, where the ambition was a complete integration of art, architecture and nature. But among the sketches is one sheet featuring reflections on the interplay between the arts, where suddenly the word 'film' stands out, enhanced by underlining. From this grew a number of drawings that develop cinematic spaces, a grand hall, monumental stairs and a garden.

The drawings point towards an approach that isn't truly resolved until much later in Larsen's work, as he describes it himself in his note, 'where one is either moved – or moves oneself – through time and space'.

Through his life, he often recounted how cinema played a large role in his personal artistic development. He was a connoisseur of not just American and European films but also Russian and Japanese classics, far beyond the best-known ones.

Sketch,
Gold Medal competition

Youth 40

Sketches of monumental stairs

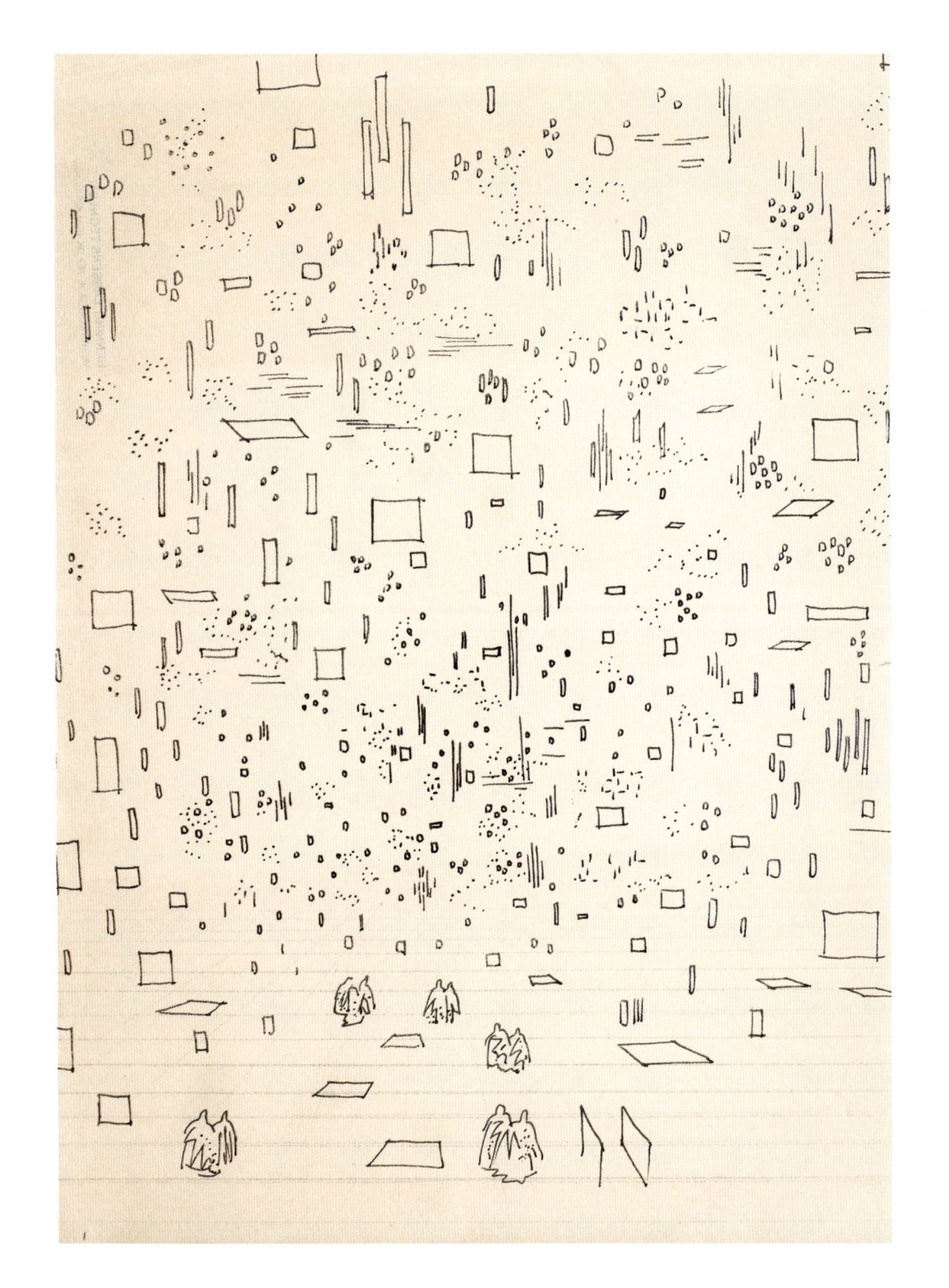

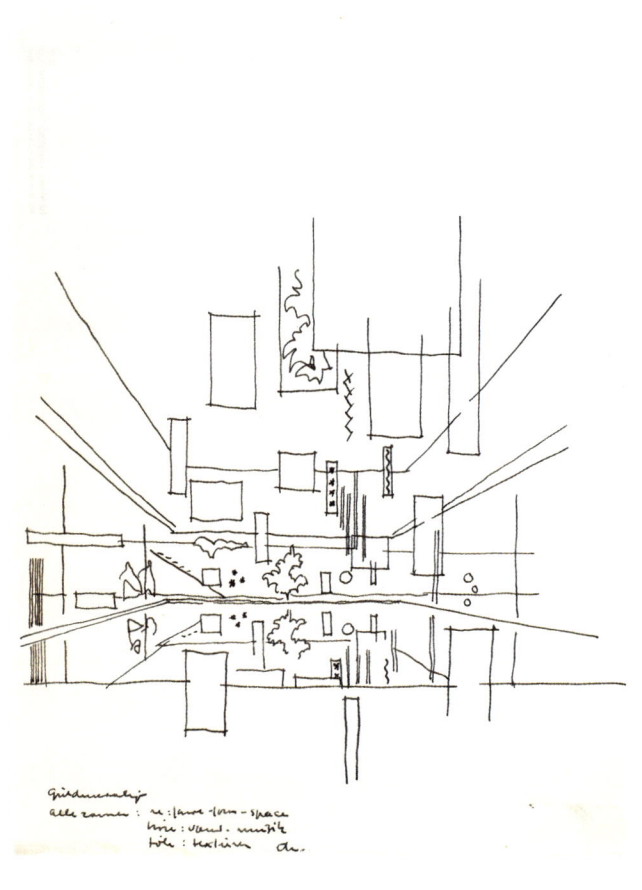

Sketches, Gold Medal competition

Youth 42

Illustration: From his early years there are a number of undated drawings where Larsen experiments with graphic art and painting, using different tools and materials. The vivacious line he developed early in life with inspiration from Le Corbusier and Axel Nygaard was a constant throughout his life, but he also made attempts with bolder lines and dramatic framing, elements that would reappear later in life.

Experimental sketch

The beginning of the office

The beginning of the office
Hvidovre Hospital

Hvidovre Hospital

The competition for Hvidovre Hospital, in 1963, wasn't a big success for the young office. It only brought in a purchase. But the sketches and the project are interesting because they were clearly created in dialogue with Henning Larsen's friends and former partners Gert Bornebusch, Max Brüel and Jørgen Selchau, who were then working on Herlev Hospital, a project Larsen was originally invited to participate in. Henning Larsen was particularly fond of Max Brüel and admired his talent, and it is easy to imagine that their professional dialogue continued after the end of the collaboration. At the same time, it is very clear that the drawings indicate a strong vision and intention now Larsen is the boss in his own office.

After the Second World War, hospitals were developed into very large and complex assignments, often the size of a whole town. Planning the infrastructure and the integration of technology were and are still a significant part of the design task. This can be seen in the sketches from the project; they interchange between analytical drawings that examine the site, exploration of different plan typologies, diagrams of the infrastructure, and spatial drawings exploring the sculptural and monumental potential of the structures.

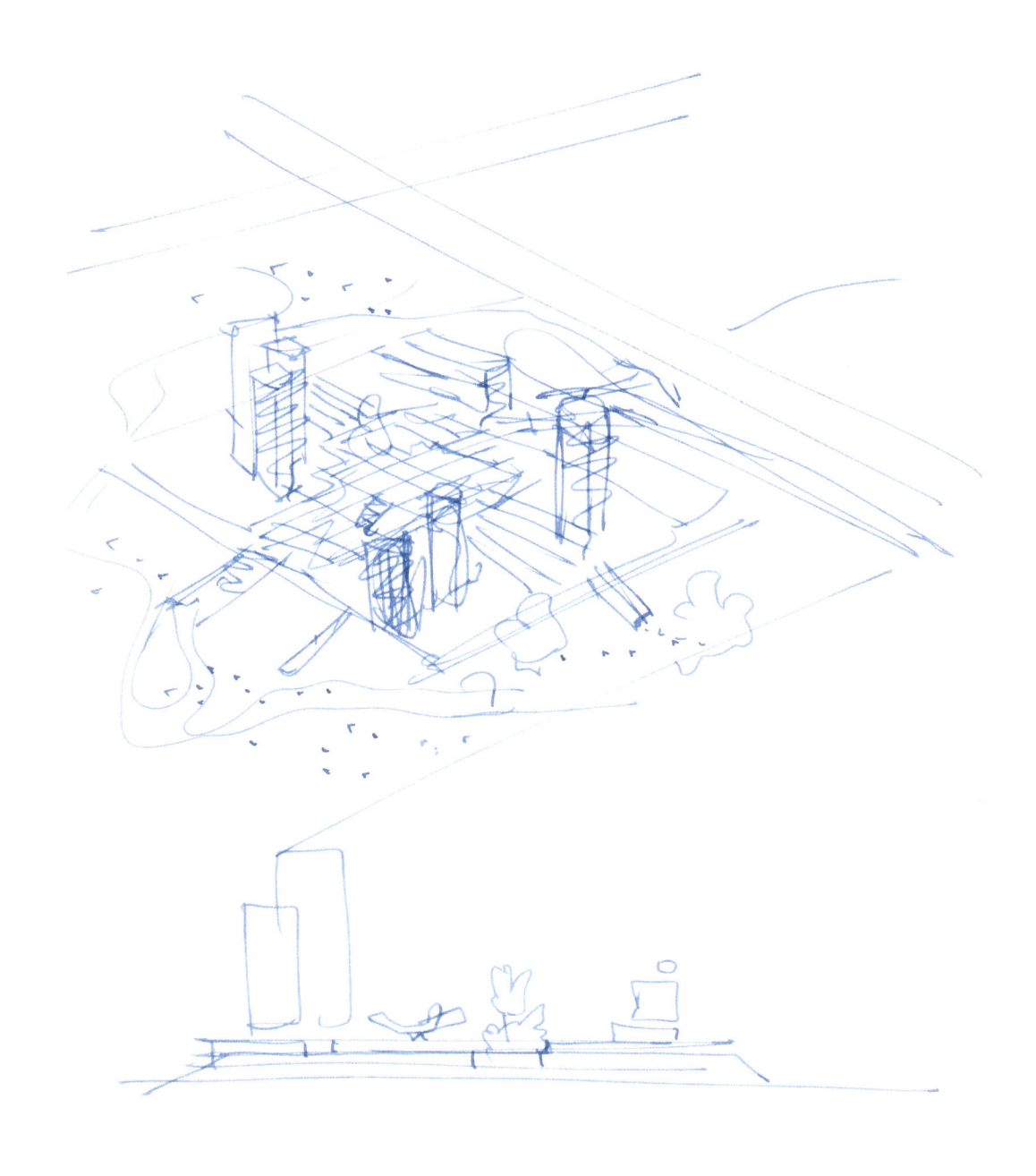

The beginning of the office
Hvidovre Hospital

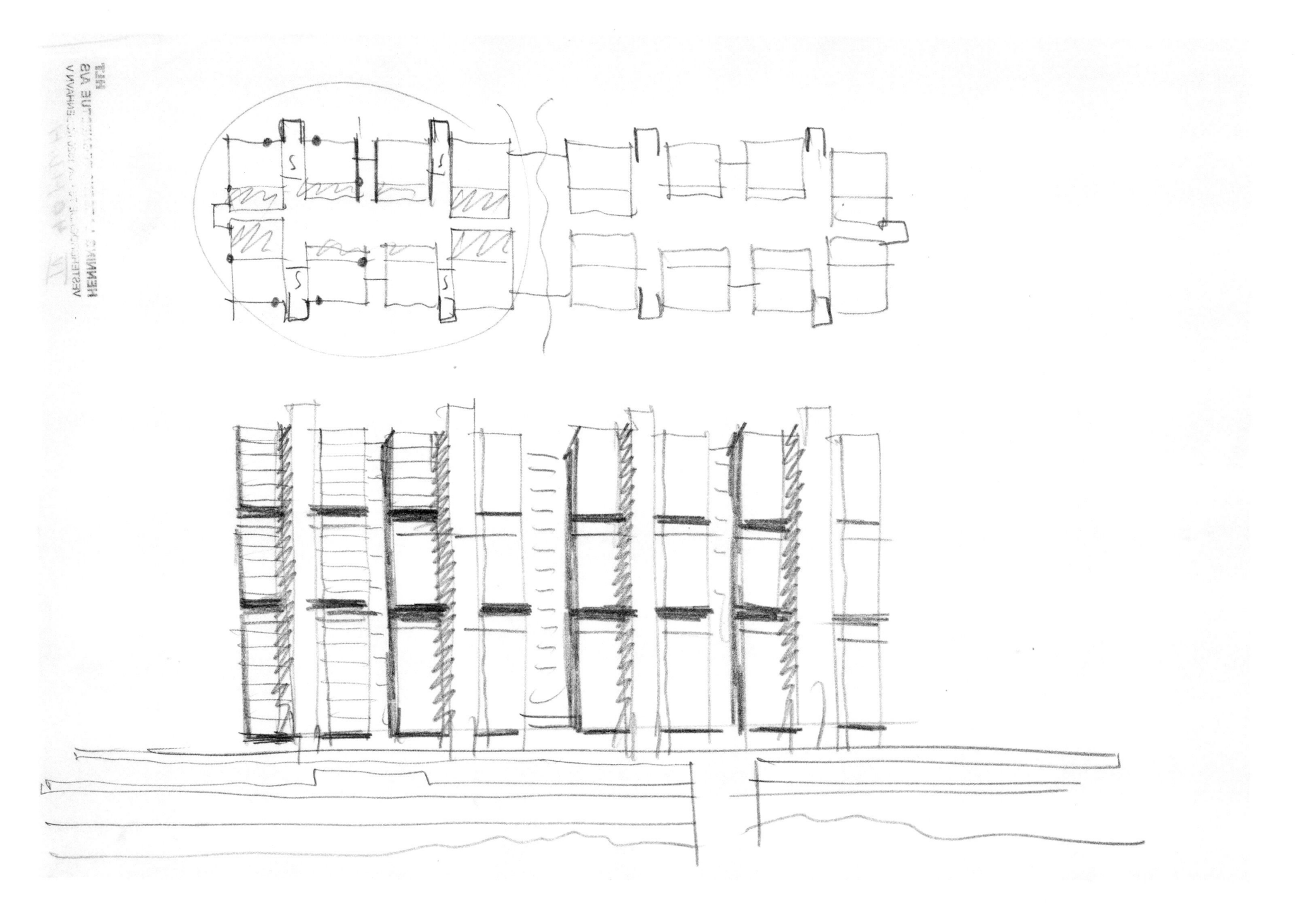

49

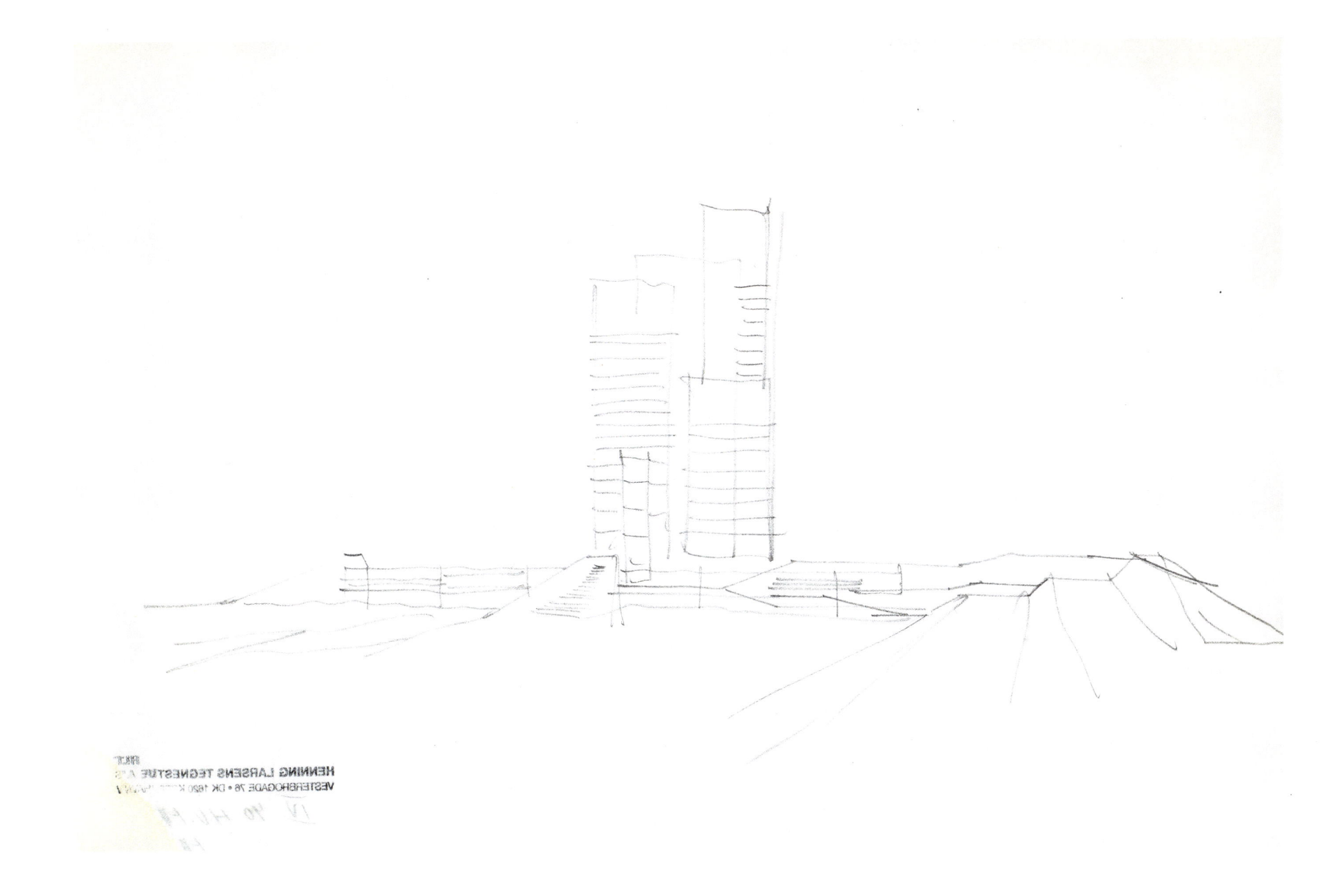

The beginning of the office
Freie Universität

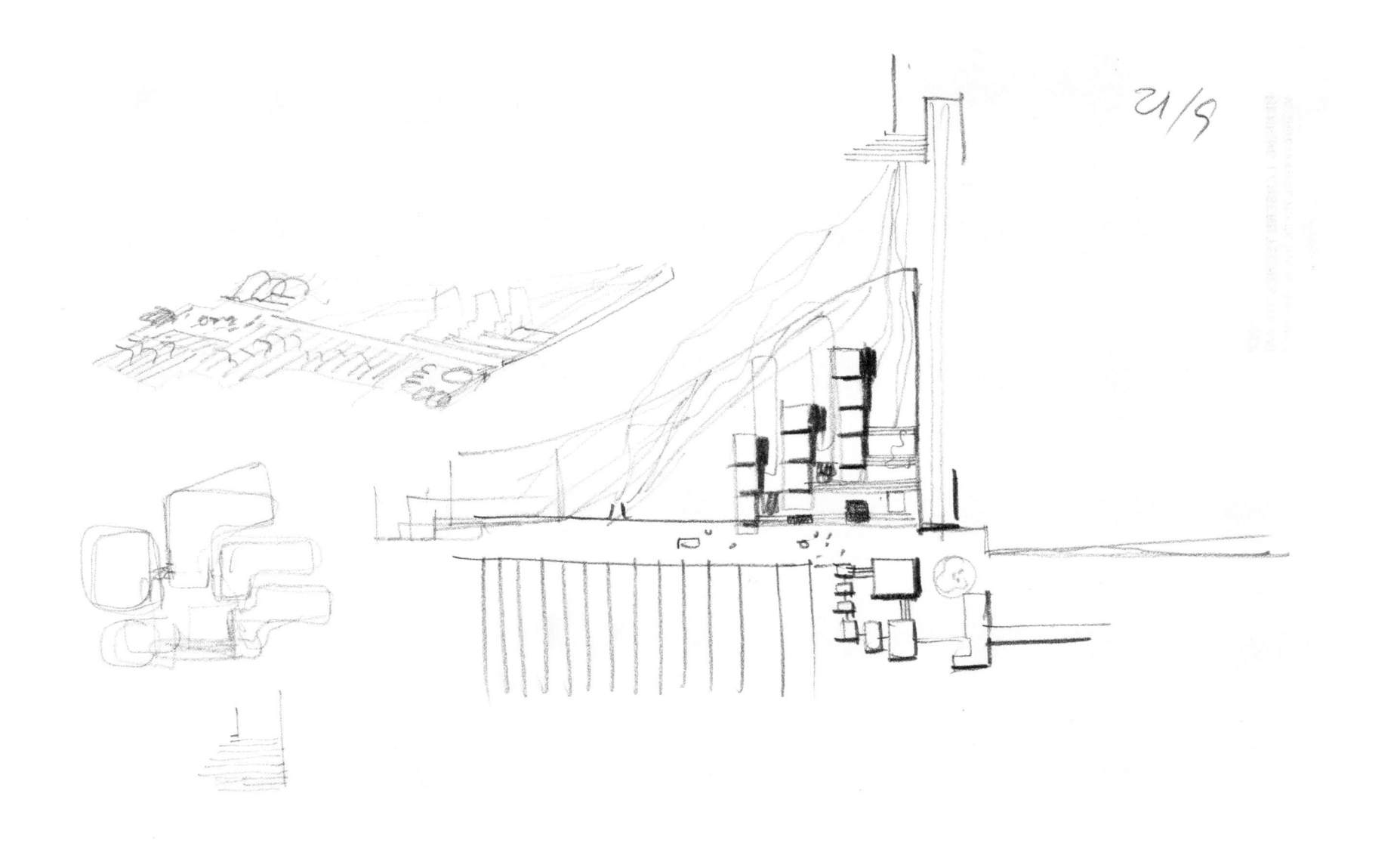

Freie Universität

In 1963, the office entered a competition for the Freie Universität in Berlin. The project became Henning Larsen's international breakthrough, despite the project being awarded second prize. Here, the structuralist ideas and methods from London created the foundations of the project, from city and landscape planning to concrete details. As in the Hvidovre project, the sketches alternate between the structural/diagrammatic and the formal/monumental. In these sketches we also find traces of another aspect of an architect's work: managing the project. Between sketches of monumental auditoriums are lists of tasks, divided between the team. The concept that one architect alone can create large projects like this university is pure fantasy. Architecture is teamwork, and making the team work in a way that enhances the artistic vision is an important part of the job. As the office grew, Henning Larsen no longer took part in the actual drafting work. The large drawings could take several days to produce, and it wouldn't be practical for the team manger to be tied to one desk and one drawing. Instead, the freehand sketches began to play an even more significant role as communicators of the main intentions in the project and as a tool for dialogue at the desks. Larsen spoke very quietly and seldom; the drawings did the main talking.

In 1976 construction began on the part of the university the office had been asked to build within the framework of the winning entry.

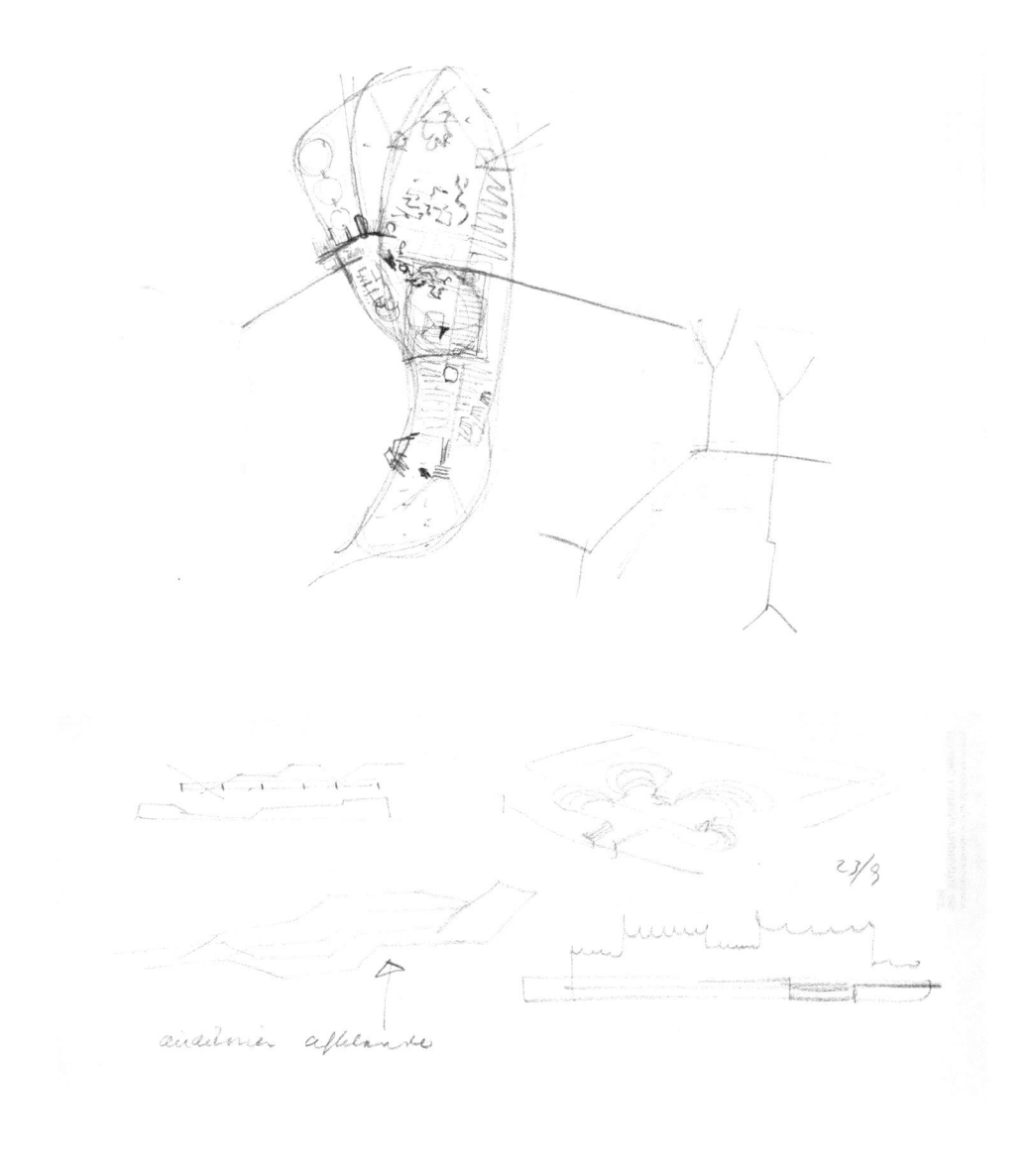

The beginning of the office
Freie Universität

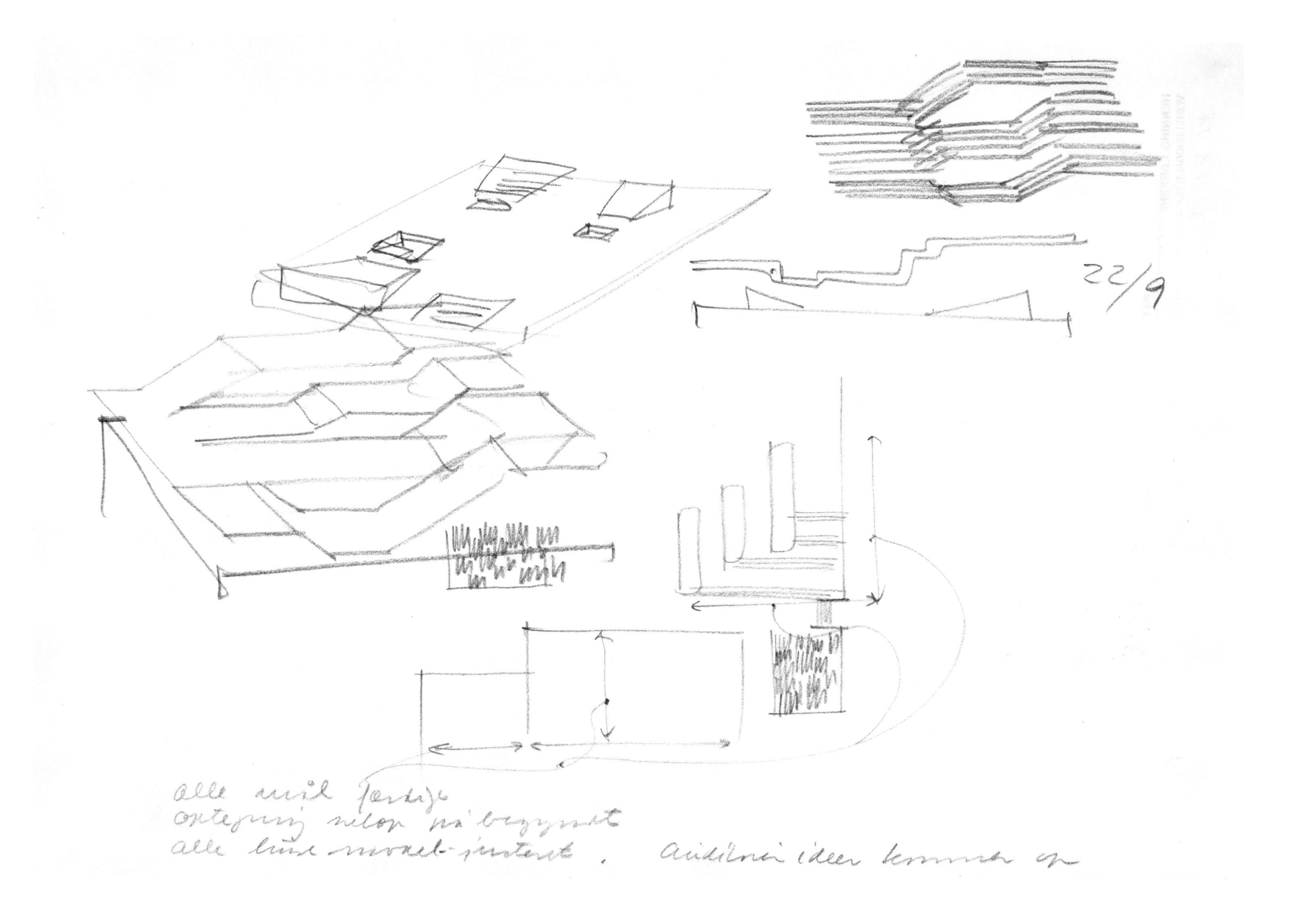

53

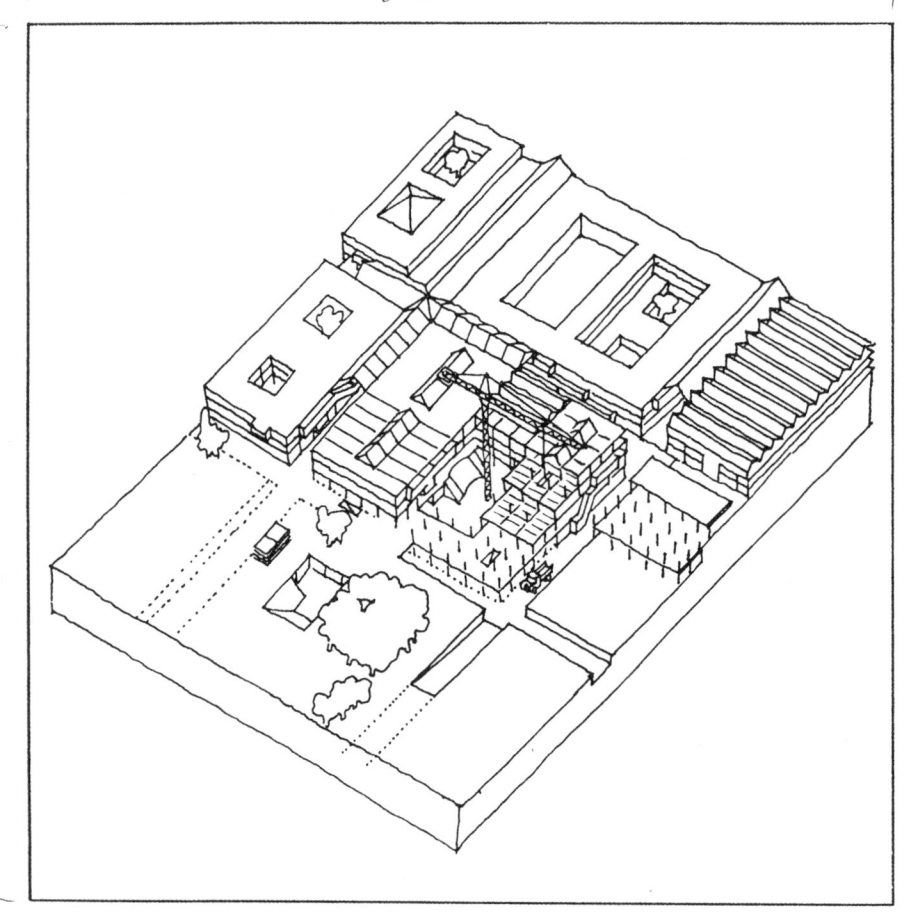

Byggeprocessen er igang. Man ser forholdet mellem køreveje, parkering, de delvis overdækkede fodgængergader og den indtil 3 etager høje bygningsstruktur. (maximal højde for trappebetjente bygninger).

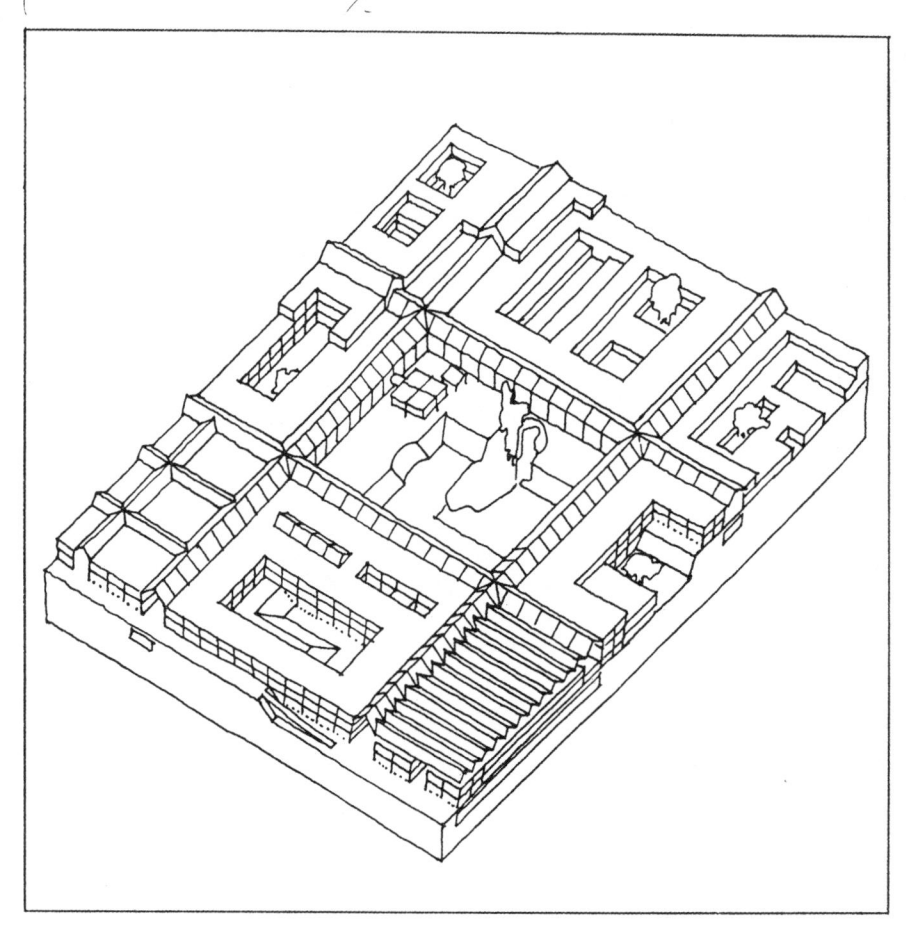

Naturen er indesluttet i gårde og fuldstændigt kultiveret. Gaderne og en del af de interne gårde er glasoverdækkede. Forneden et eksempel på en større glasoverdækning med mulighed for friere rumdisponering i takt med evt. ændrede behov.

The beginning of the office
PH Competition

PH Competition

The PH competition in 1964 was an open-vision competition about the urban renewal of Nørrebro, an inner-city neighbourhood in Copenhagen known at the time for its blight and squalor. The aim of the competition was not to find a realistic proposal for the renewal of the area but to present visions of the city for the future.

  The project spans from regional plan to individual dwelling and is worked through on all levels. There are many sketches, detailed drawings and almost illegible notes. Both in the final project and in the sketches, daylight plays a significant role. Daylight was an important welfare element in housing and regulated in different ways throughout the twentieth century in Denmark. At a latitude of 55°, Copenhagen has long, dark winters and summers where the sun only sets for a few hours. For mental and physical health reasons, every home needs daylit rooms all year round, and even in the 1960s the poor quality and high price of artificial lighting meant this was less than optimal for many daily tasks. So attention to the quality of daylight was a basic consideration for a Danish architect. But it is clear from the sketches and notes for this competition that Henning Larsen intended to bring it a step further.

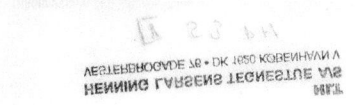

The project was openly inspired by the masterplan for Tokyo, by Kenzo Tange. There is a direct mention of it in one of the sketches for the project, and it is interesting to see how Henning Larsen was up to date with international trends at a time where the distribution of knowledge was much slower than today.

In Denmark, the concept of terraced apartments over a tier of parking garages was realized at Murergården in Nørrebro, by Niels J. Holm in 1975, and at Farum Midtpunkt, by the firm Fællestegnestuen in 1970–75. Whether those offices found their inspiration in Larsen's competition project or from international sources is not known.

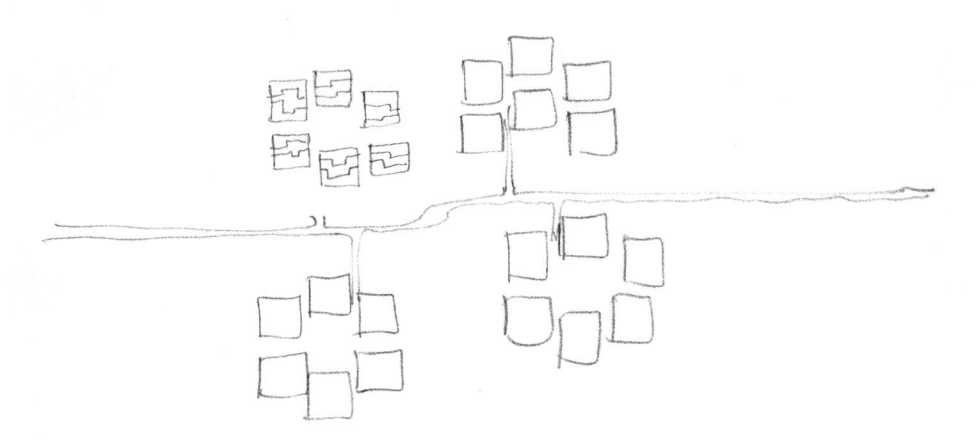

situationsplan for et større område

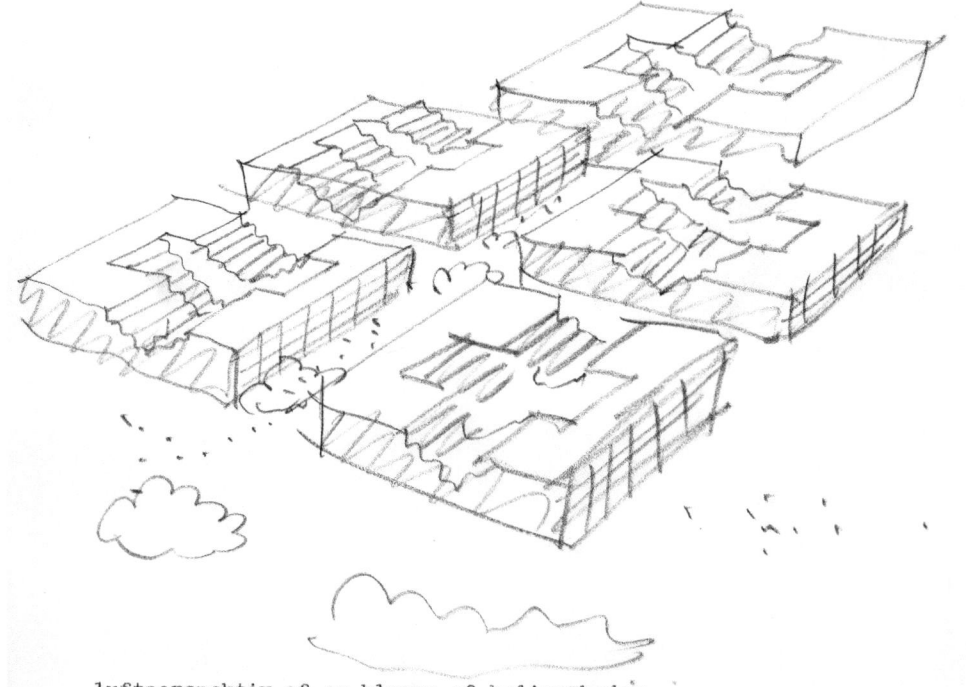

luftperspektiv af en klynge af boligenheder

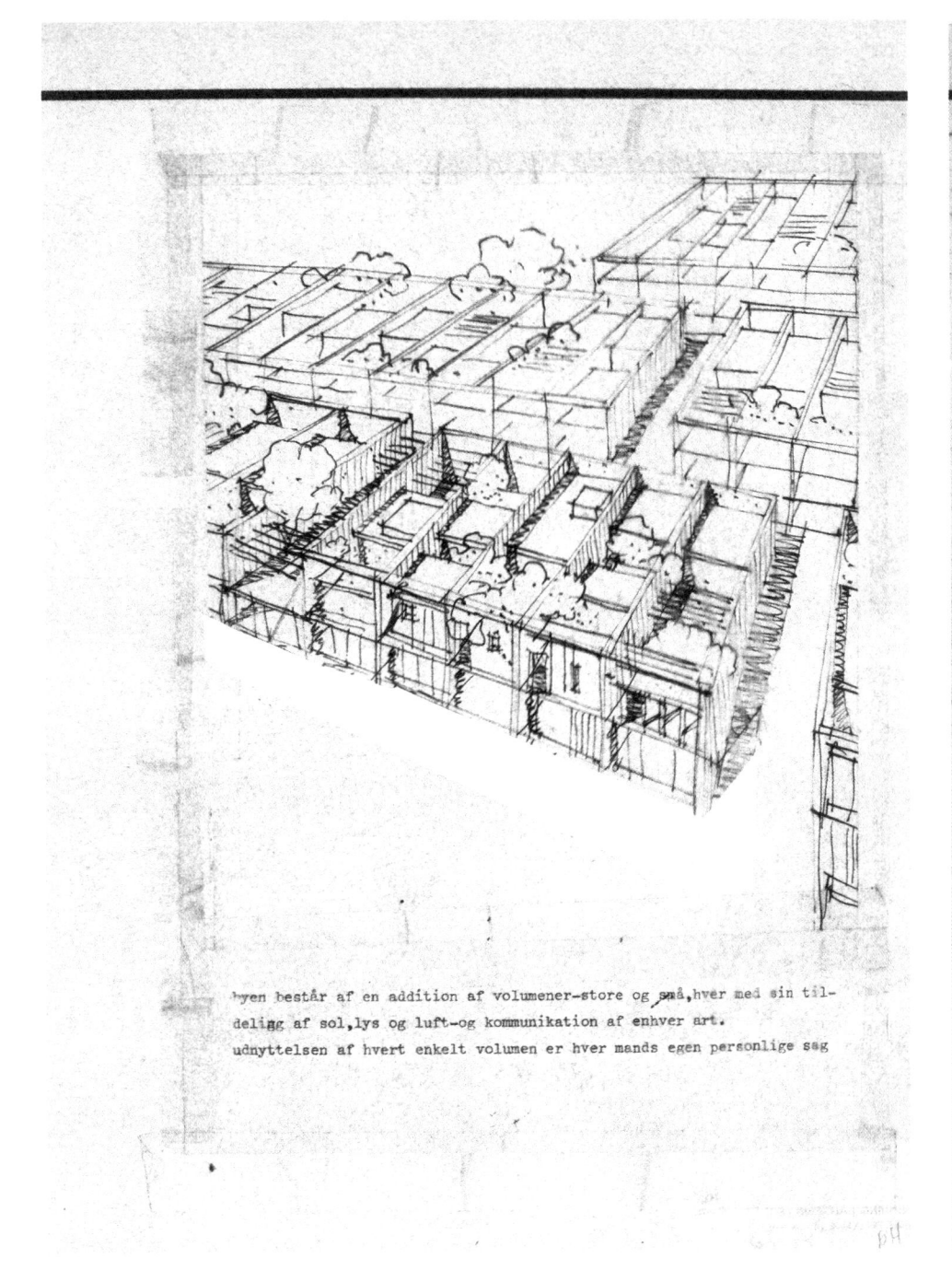

byen består af en addition af volumener-store og små, hver med sin tildeling af sol, lys og luft-og kommunikation af enhver art.
udnyttelsen af hvert enkelt volumen er hver mands egen personlige sag

IDE   P-H. Kouleur.

øresund

boliger med udsigt

bydannelser der hviler i sig selv
ingen udsigt

bykvarter der hviler
i sig selv

boliger med udsigt

The beginning of the office
PH Competition

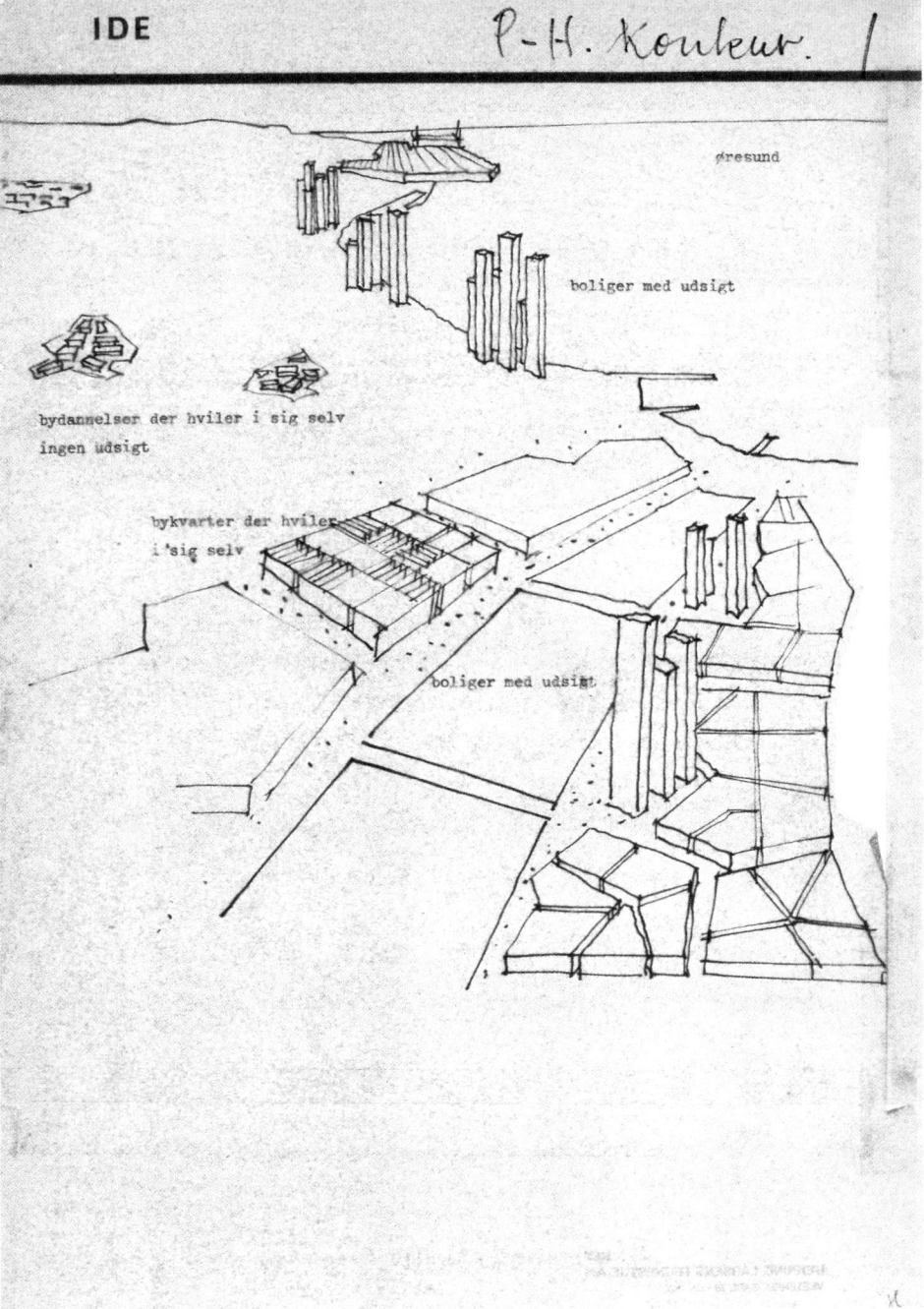

The beginning of the office
Industriens Hus

Industriens Hus

The competition for the Industriens Hus (House of Industry) took place in 1965. The site between Tivoli, the Town Hall Square and Vesterbrogade has puzzled architects to this day. How does one handle the transition between the relatively small and incredibly idyllic amusement garden and the heavily trafficked main thoroughfare? Larsen suggested a radical and somewhat harsh proposal, with five large modernistic blocks along the street. The proposal is precise and self-assured in its simplicity, but in the freehand sketches the vision is unveiled: the sombre architecture is imagined as a calm frame for the lively street scenery featuring trees and neon lights and, of course, the thousands of people in the area. For the competition presentation, formal, uninteresting perspectives were used. Perhaps the proposal could have won if these charming sketches had been used instead.

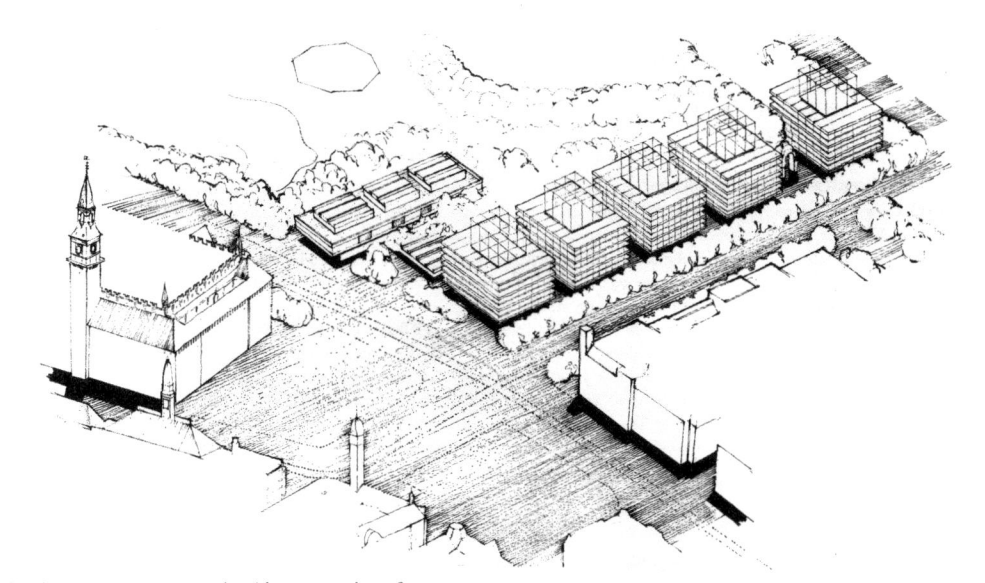

Aksonometri af Henning Larsens 2. præmieprojekt nr. 31, mrk. 34567.

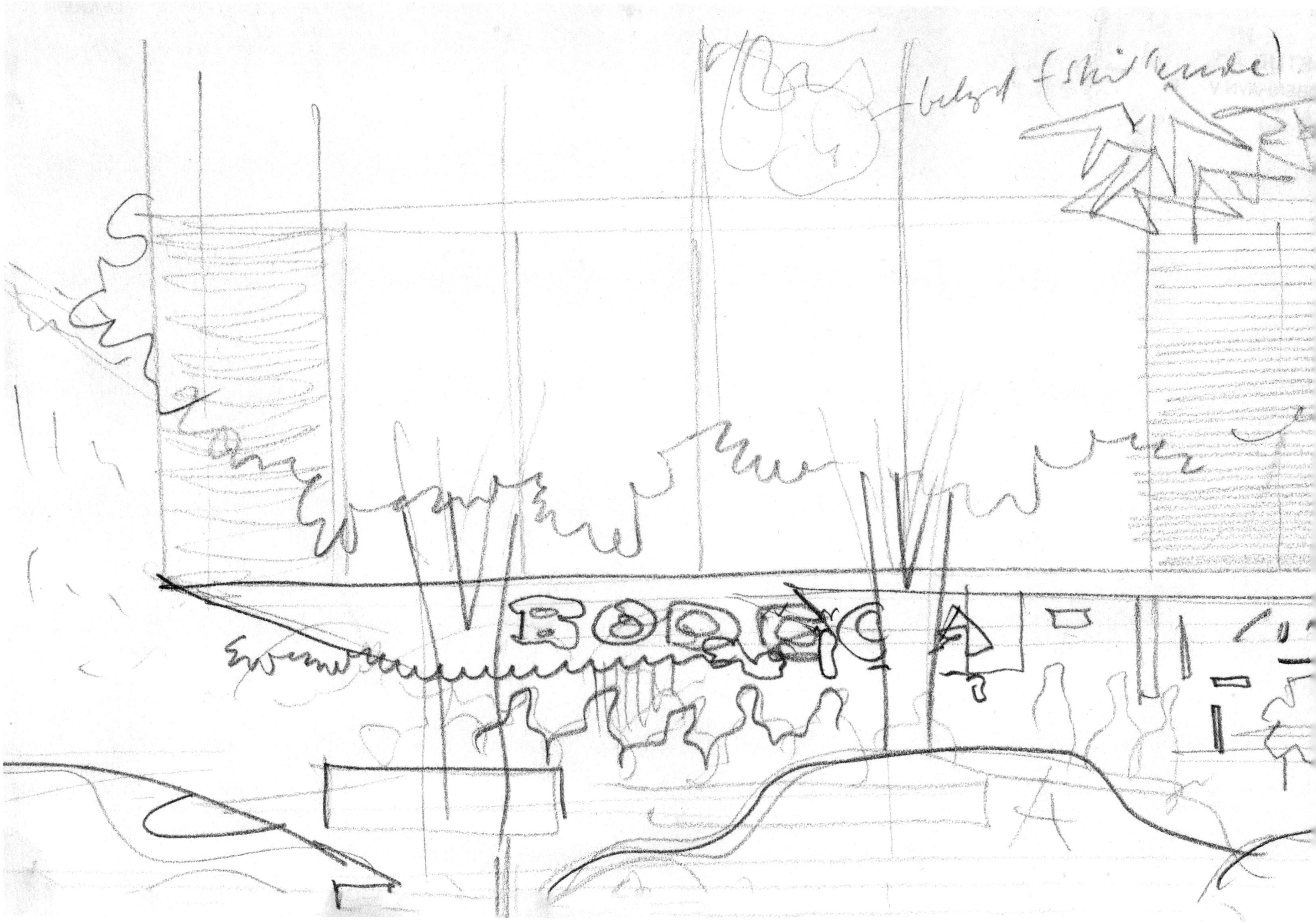

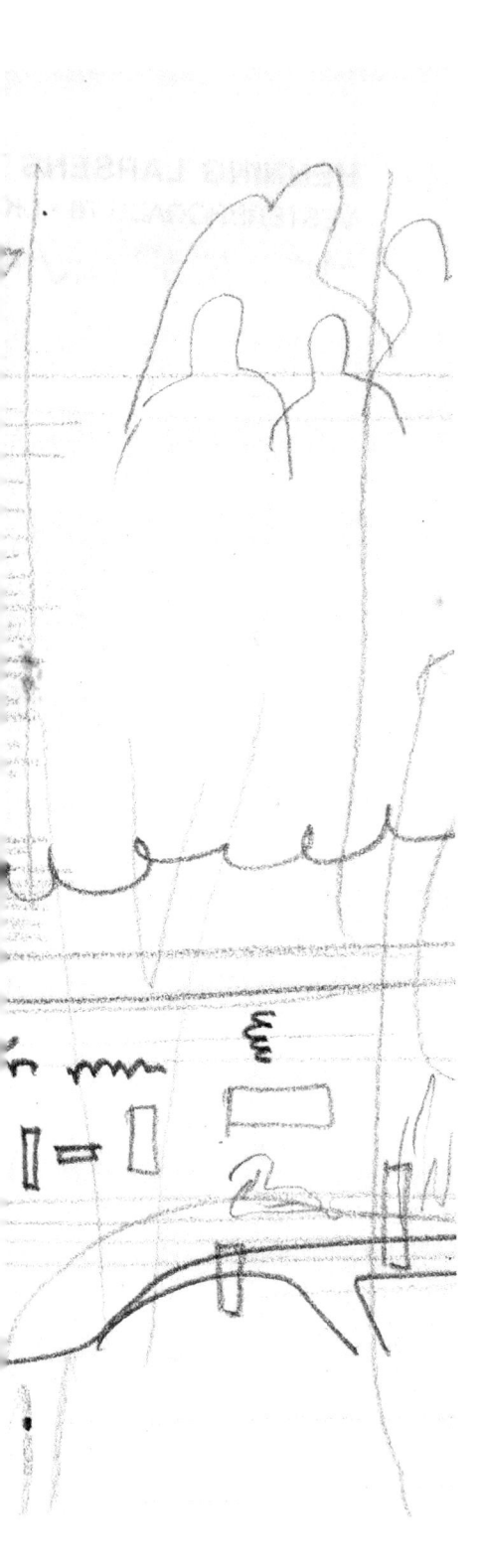

The beginning of the office
Industriens Hus

Chapel in Aarhus, 1967

The chapel and crematorium in Århus Vester Kirkegård (Aarhus Western Cemetery) was a rare task, without competition. It was completed in 1967. The sketches span from the overall site plan to details including furniture, altar, chairs and light fixtures. Some of the drawings were made with a ruler and triangle and are characteristically humble, with more weight on the trees than the building.

At the same time there are a few fascinating, riotous drawings, more like fine art than architectural design. They seem inspired by the sketches of Louis Kahn, which Larsen may have seen while he taught at Yale and Princeton in 1964–65, but there is also a likeness with the work of Danish artist Palle Nielsen.

The beginning of the office
Chapel in Aarhus, 1967

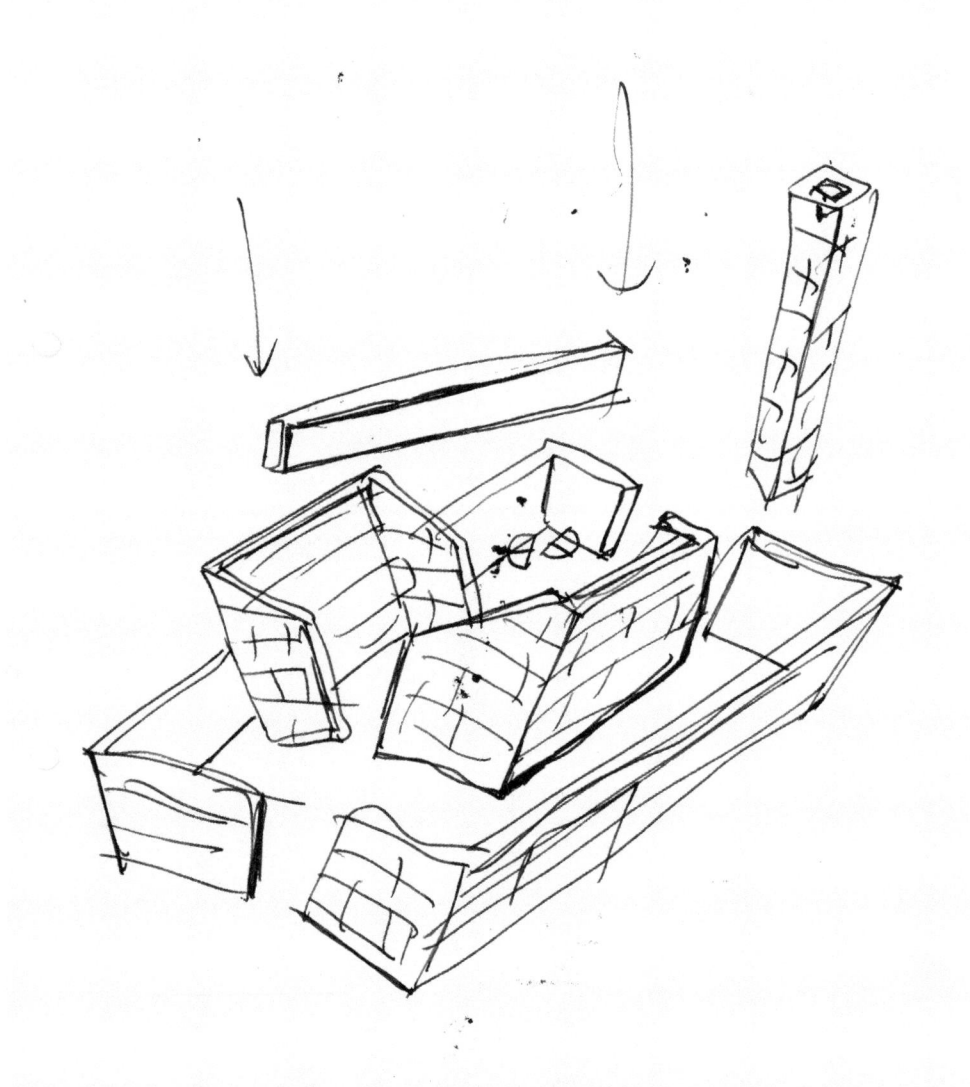

63

The beginning of the office
Chapel in Aarhus, 1967

The beginning of the office
Chapel in Aarhus, 1967

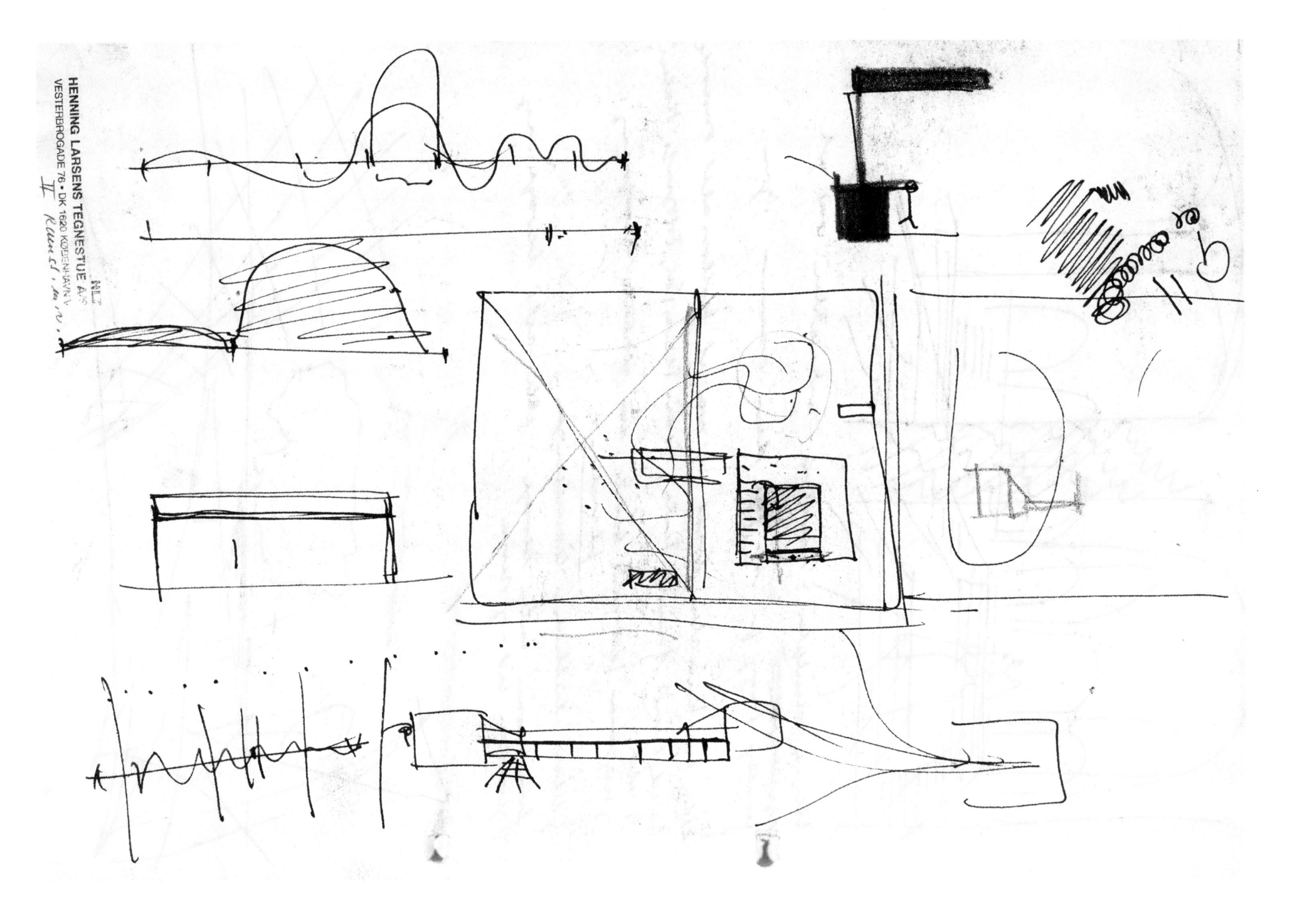

The beginning of the office
Chapel in Aarhus, 1967

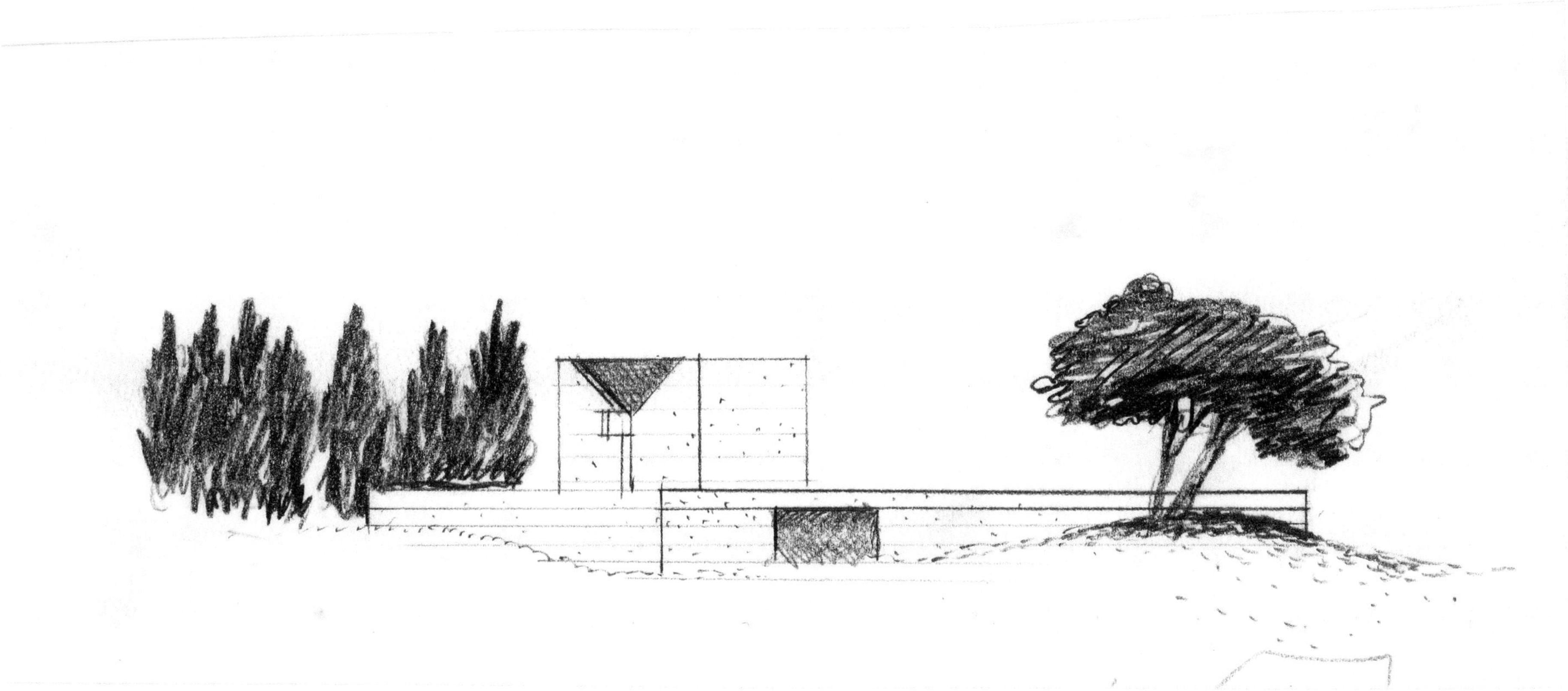

Mother Denmark

Mother Denmark

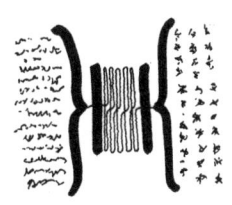

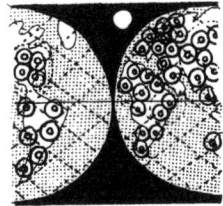

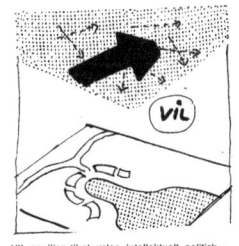

During the last years of the 1960s and the early 1970s, most of the Western world was engulfed in political and social turmoil. In Denmark, the Royal Academy of Fine Arts, as the only site of higher education in the country, was a centre of action, where the students of architecture took over management of the school and introduced free access. Henning Larsen was made full professor in 1968, just as everything broke loose, and his department 'B' became the haunt of the most radical Marxists, who even changed the name of the department to 'M' accordingly.

While Larsen later claimed that he was scared of the students and didn't understand what they wanted, because some of them wished to abandon design altogether, he must initially have felt a return to his student days in London, with Arthur Korn and the MARS group as mentors. Now he was the mentor, and this is probably a fitting angle of interpretation of the graphic series *Mor Danmark*, from 1970. The series was printed in the avant-garde journal *A + B*, which was edited by Troels Andersen. Troels Andersen was a co-founder of the Eksperimenterende Kunstskole, or Eks-Skole (Experimental Art School), with artist Poul Gernes. The school was an important hub for the avant-garde of the 1960s in Denmark, and *A + B* was a direct heir of the other avant-garde journals Andersen had edited. There were articles about the Situationists and other radical movements within art and architecture as well as about politics and planning. The journal was richly illustrated with graphic works by the Eks-Skole circle of artists, among others.

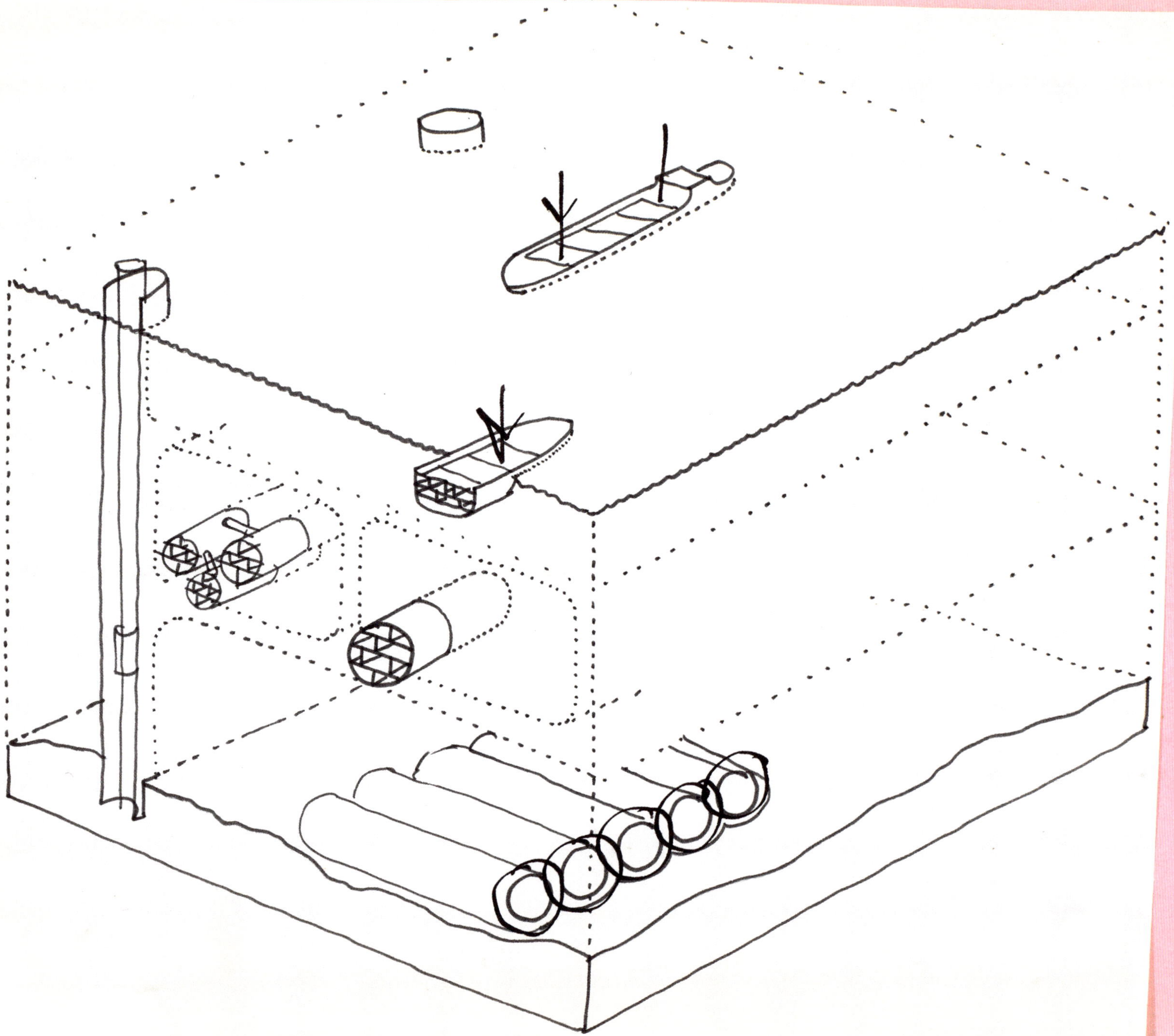

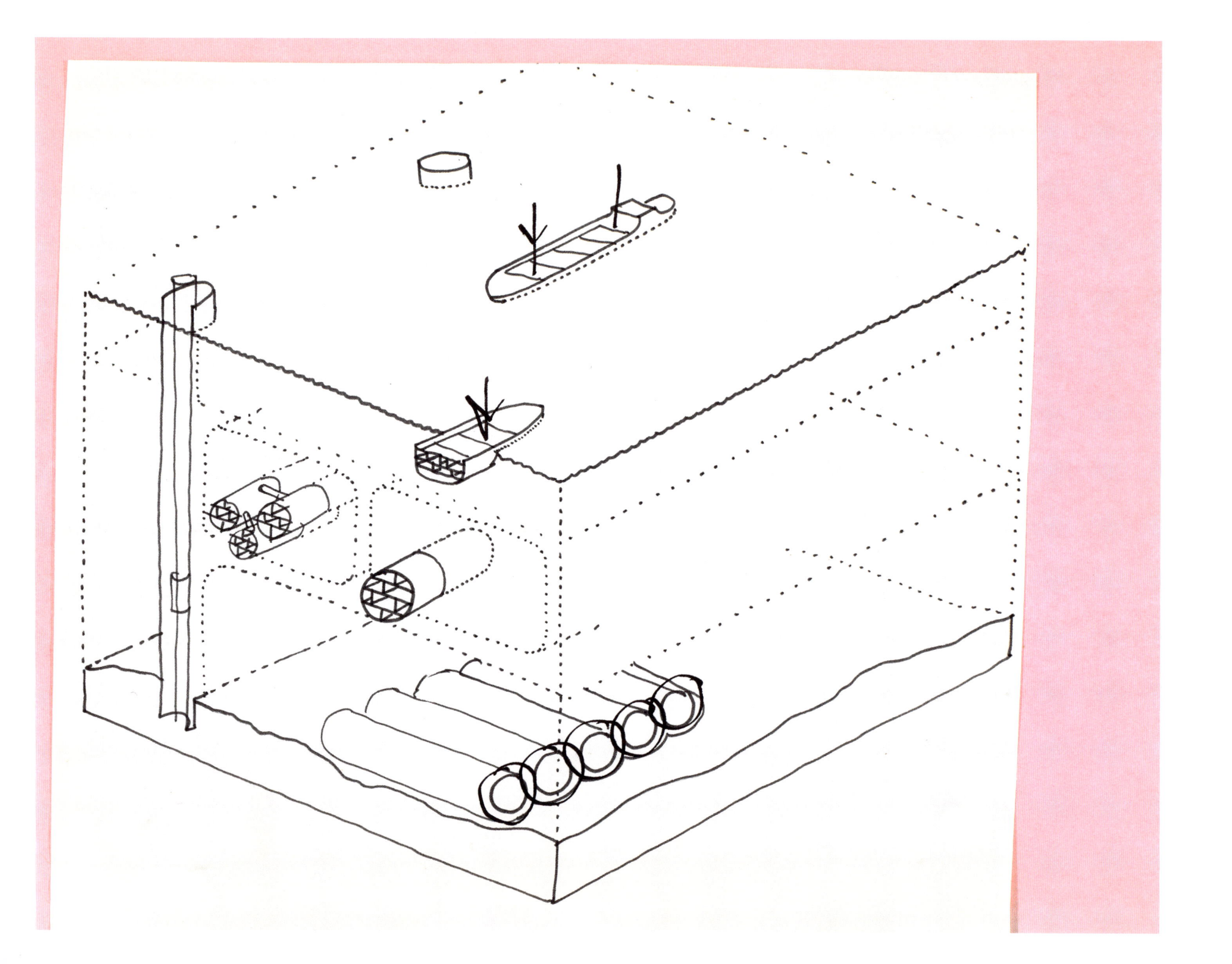

The content of the series is a type of MARS-plan Marxist analysis and interpretation of the future potential of Denmark, but what makes it special is the graphic presentation, little squares of line drawings that interchange between diagram and illustration, punctuated by larger images. The many sketches for this project show how it was developed, with the analytical, structural approach from the MARS plan as the point of departure, and then unfolded in monumental structures that are more typical of the time (ca. 1970). The lightness and almost humorous tone of the drawings partly hide the centralistic intention so one almost doesn't notice the contrast to the more anarchic projects in the rest of the journal. The graphic series is also the first time Larsen seriously presented a project in his own hand. While there had been some vignettes in earlier projects, the descriptive perspectives had mostly been more formal constructions, made by others on the project teams.

Mother Denmark

Three projects in conversation

University of Trondheim, 1970

During the 1960s, both society as a whole and Henning Larsen had changed their understanding of what a university should be. The competition for the Freie Universität in Berlin had set a new agenda, in which the large university was interpreted as a naturally evolved provincial town rather than a monument. The most important thing now was the structure, and specifically the potential for organic growth within that structure. Here, the conceptual sketch was a natural conveyor of the intention of the project's openness.

Even after winning first prize, Henning Larsen continued to explore the project in sketches, from the overall plan to principles for structural elements. In his book *Arkitekt Henning Larsen* from 1996, Nils Ole Lund quotes the Norwegian architect, Per Knudsen, who had worked on the university project for decades: 'He came here at least once a month and often stayed for a couple of days. We had intense and creative workshops lasting all day and all night, and during such sessions he would produce countless very specific sketches. This form of leadership was probably primarily a form of design management. He didn't come to tell us how to do things, rather to show us how things should be done.'

A pastel drawing, typical for this period, indicates another new movement: the postmodern. All the way back during his student days, Larsen had been experimenting with graphic expressions and different media, but these drawings remained private. Now the colourful and playful drawings would become part of the project. A drawing like this one is not really a project drawing; it is more an architectural fantasy depicting the atmosphere Henning Larsen was aiming for in the project, a dreamy vision of the city, the light and the mountains in the distance.

Three projects in conversation
University of Trondheim, 1970

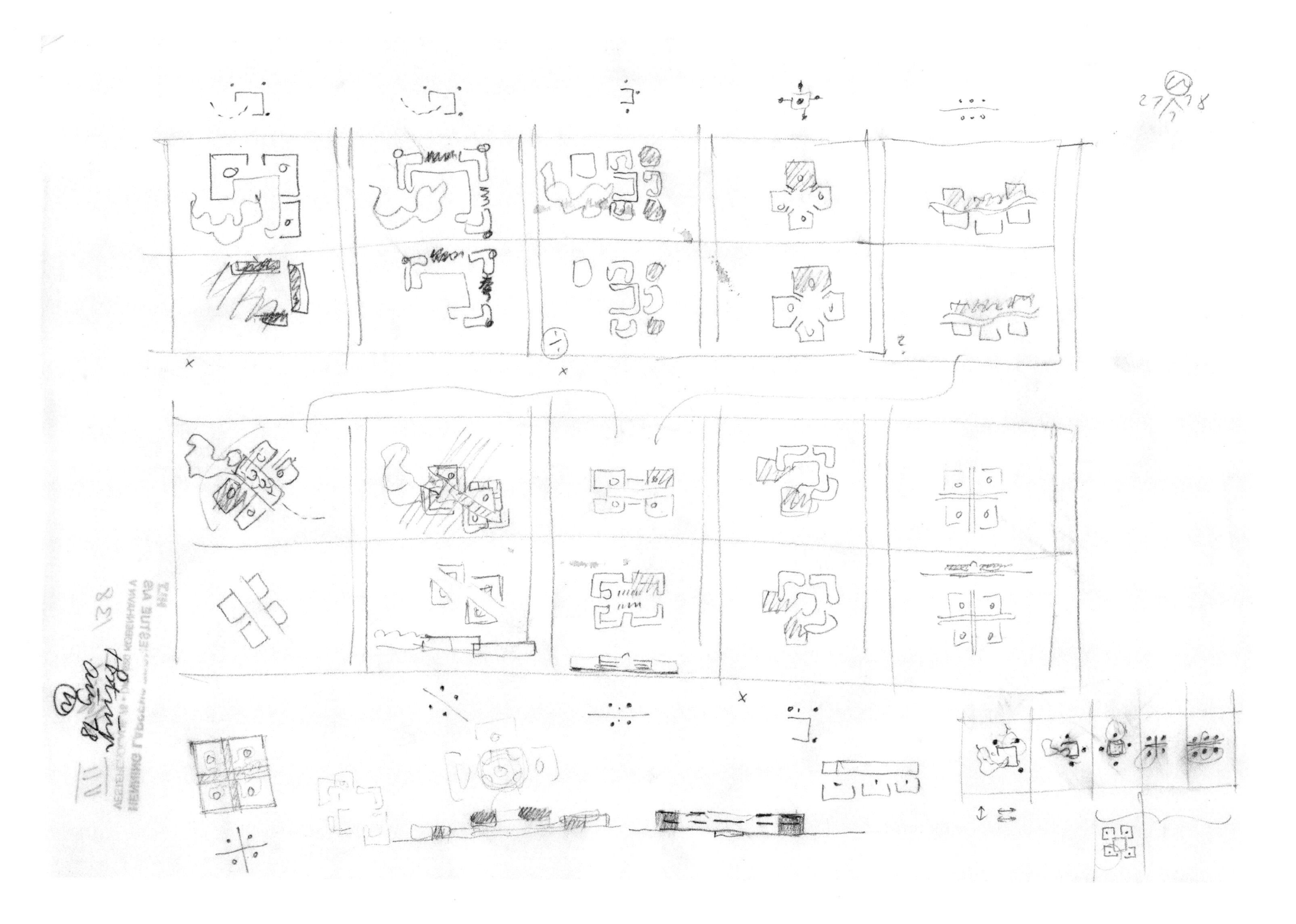

Three projects in conversation
Høje-Taastrup Amtsgymnasium, 1978

Høje-Taastrup
Amtsgymnasium, 1978

The project for a school for 16–18-year-olds takes its point of departure in an analysis of the landscape and its surroundings. The sketches show how many different typologies were tested using this analysis as their starting point. The drawings are mostly undated, but there is a clear sense of development, beginning with very open principles that are then gradually given form. The brief called for 'home areas', and the proximity to the historical Høje-Taastrup village provided the inspiration to shape the school as a cluster of 'farmyards' surrounding a common 'square', but during the process the characteristic section evolved, and the regular system was transformed into something particular, a specific place rather than an anonymous institution. This marks the beginning of a departure from the deliberate formlessness of structuralism that would be fully explored in the Saudi Arabian Ministry of Foreign Affairs.

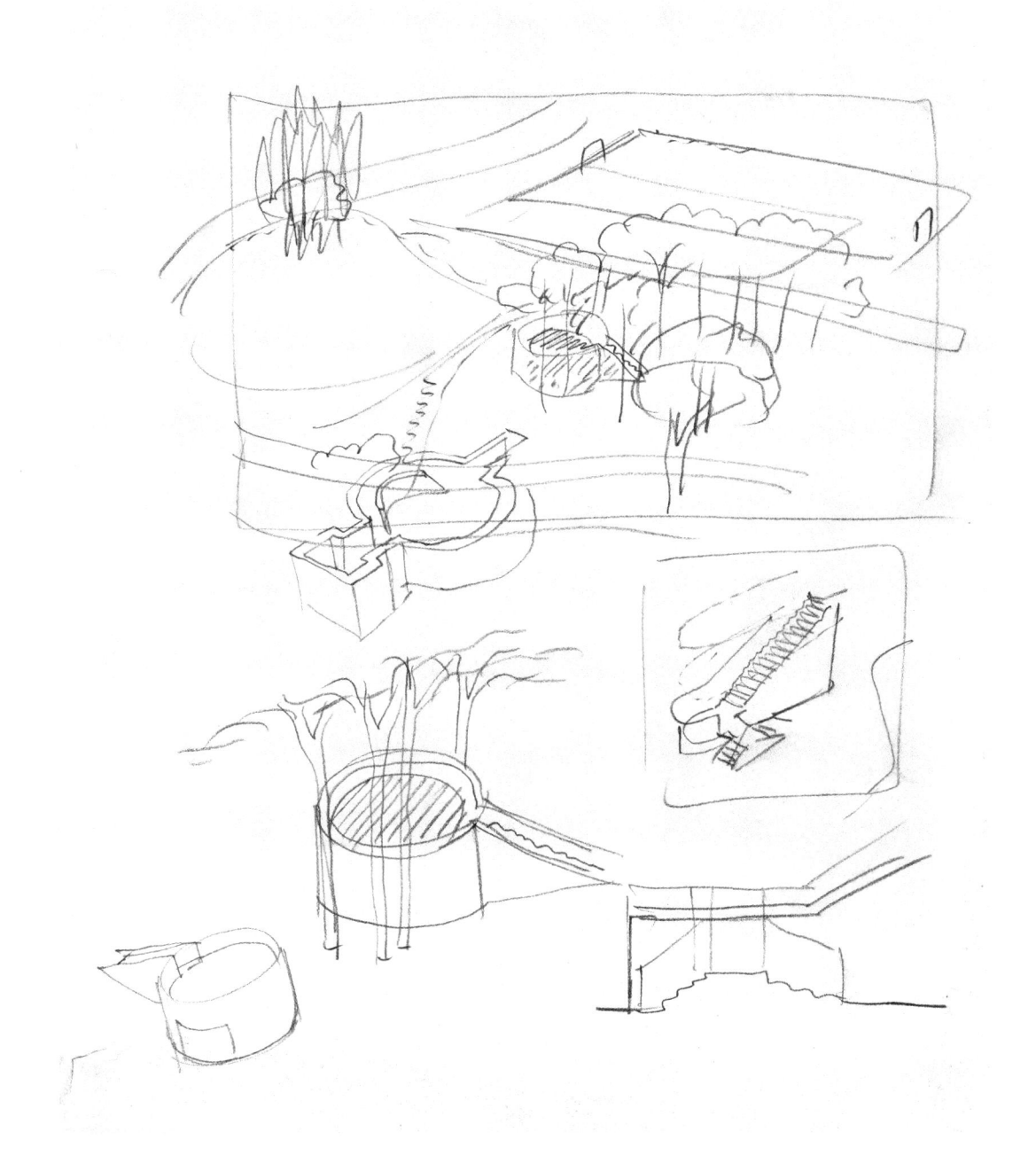

Three projects in conversation
Høje-Taastrup Amtsgymnasium, 1978

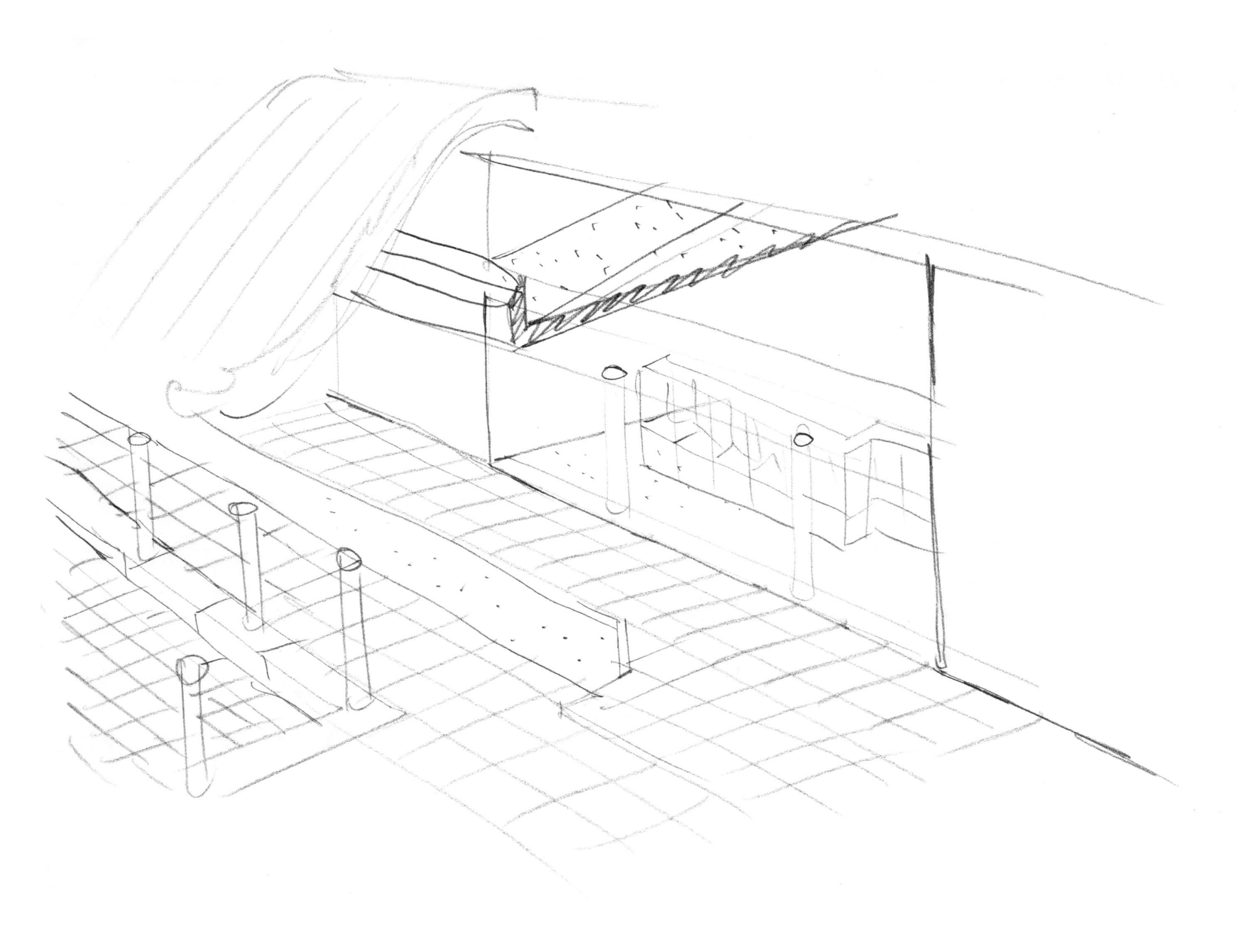

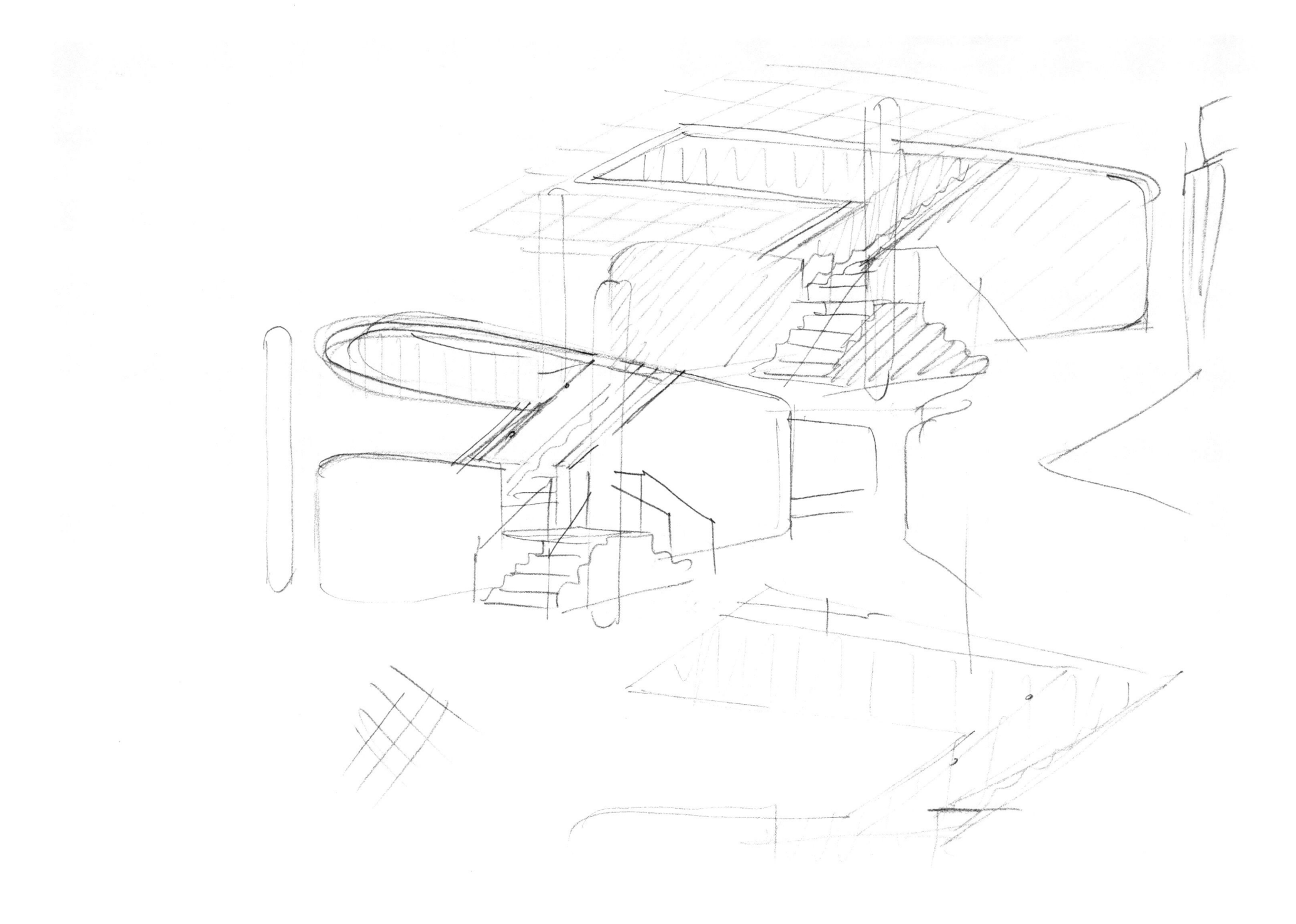

Three projects in conversation
Høje-Taastrup Amtsgymnasium, 1978

After the competition, there was a long period of development with several presentations for the municipality and the public. During this period, Henning Larsen made a set of pastel drawings that are both compositions in their own right and explorations of the potential of the section.

Gentofte Library, 1978

This library building is more formless than the contemporary school building, but it too is based on an analysis of the given site, and in the interiors of the structure there is a similar interest in place-making.

For the presentation Henning Larsen made a set of drawings filled with people and plants. In them, there is a clear intention for how to experience the building: it would be bright, light and filled with life. The drawings are a development of those created for the Industriens Hus from 1965, but while they were kept virtually private in earlier projects, now they are part of the public face of the office in the project description.

Three projects in conversation
Gentofte Library, 1978

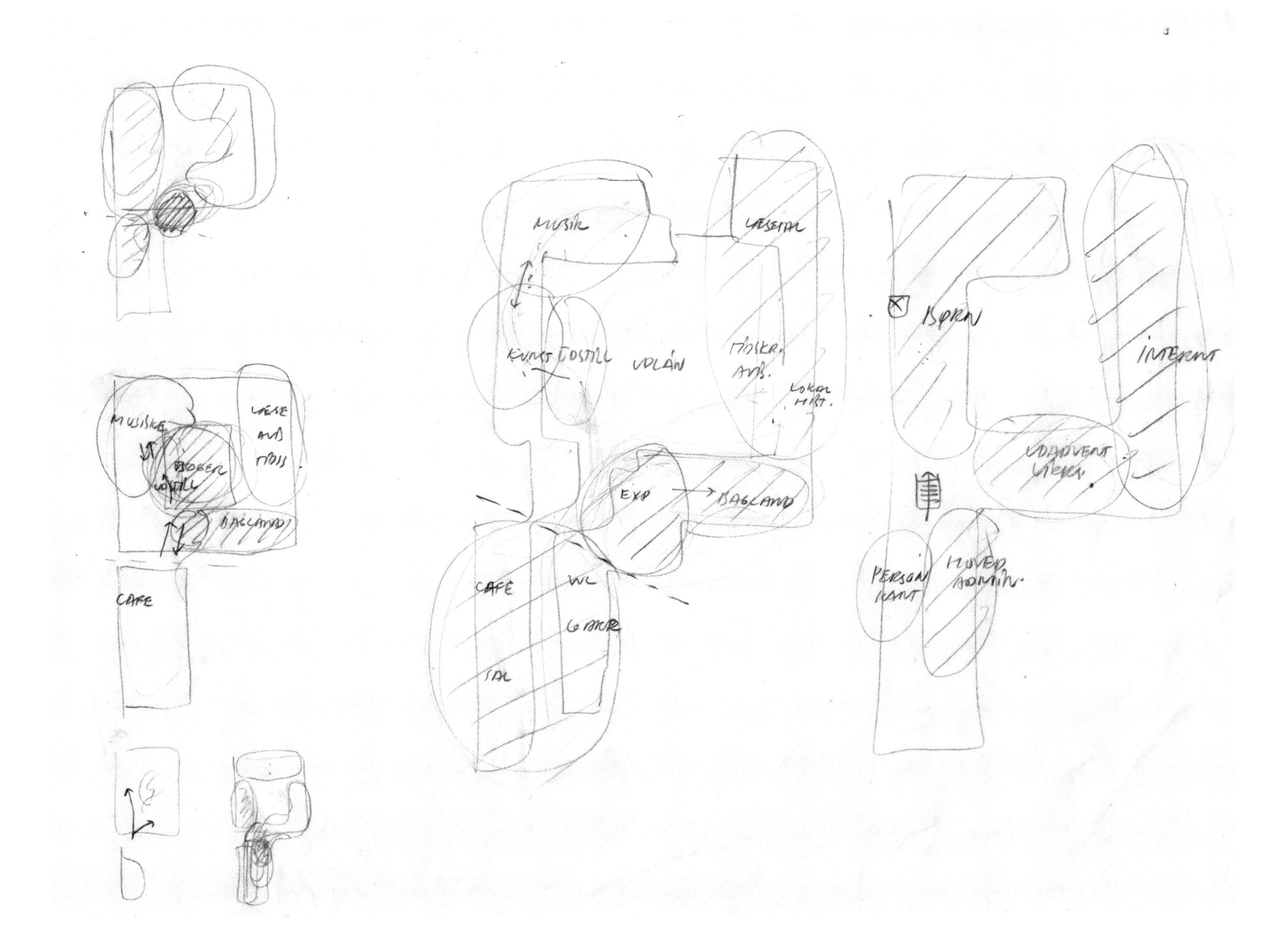

Three projects in conversation
Gentofte Library, 1978

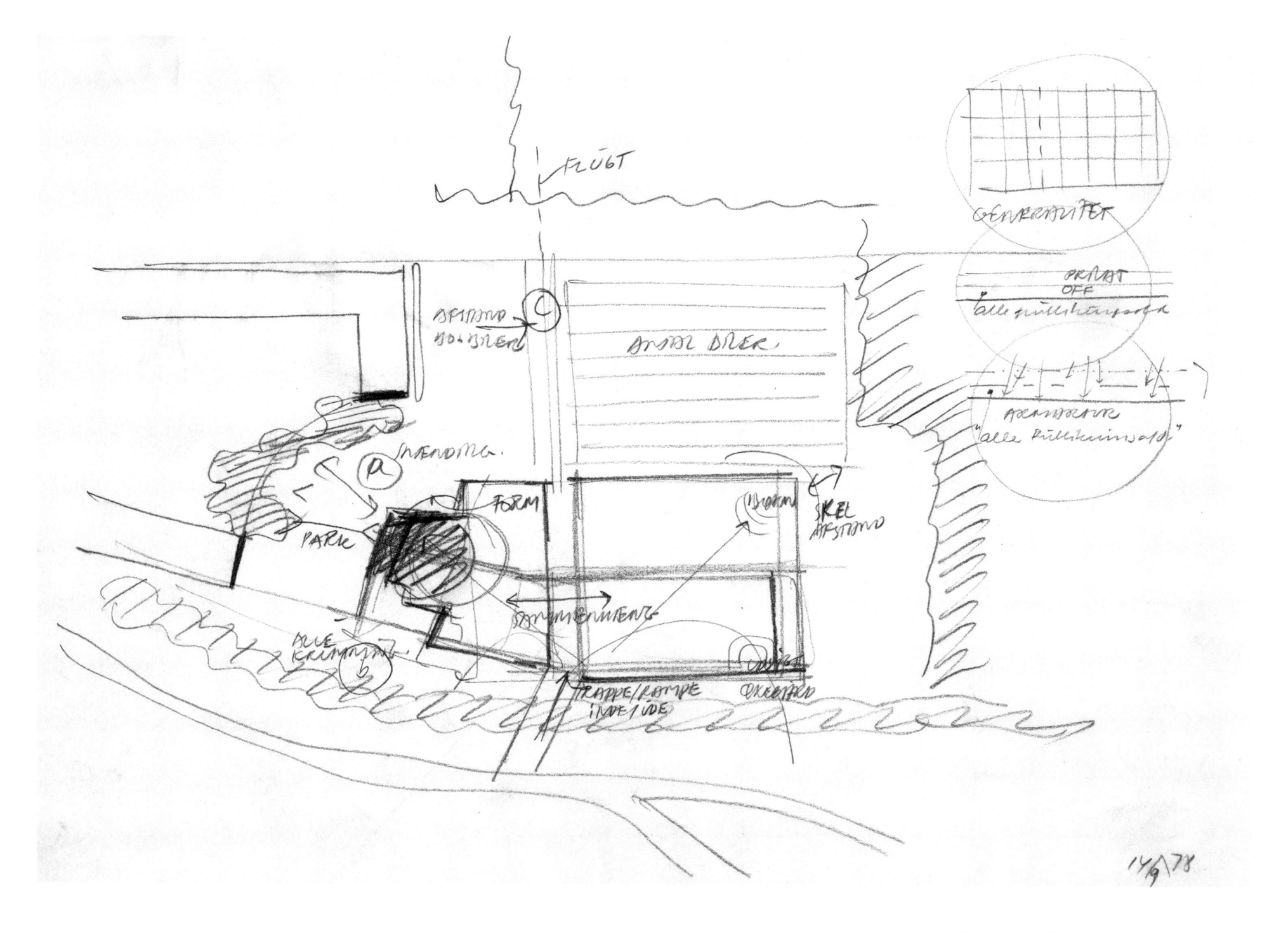

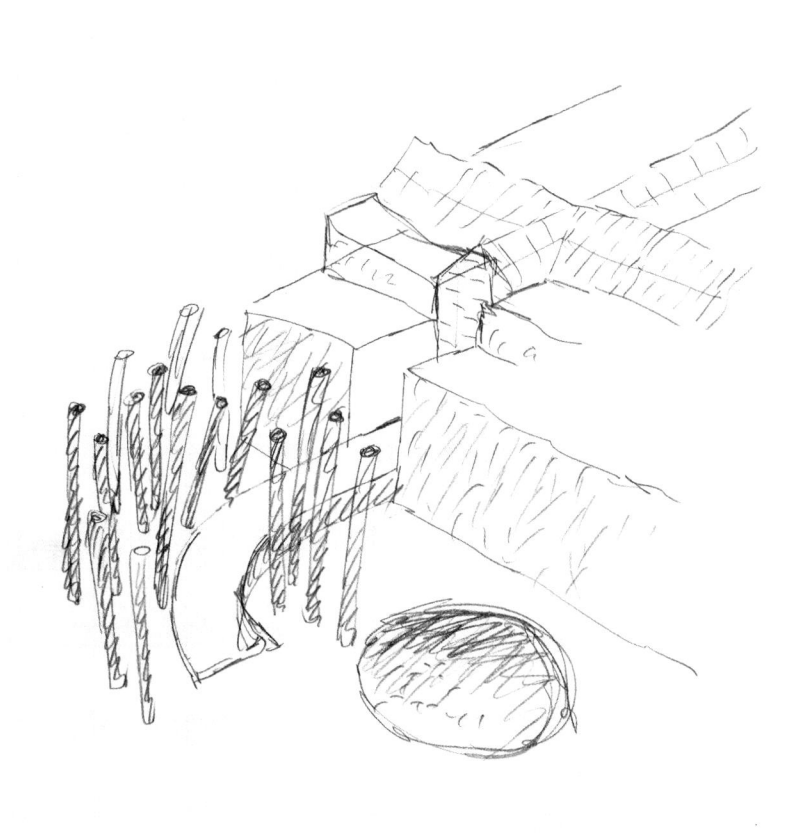

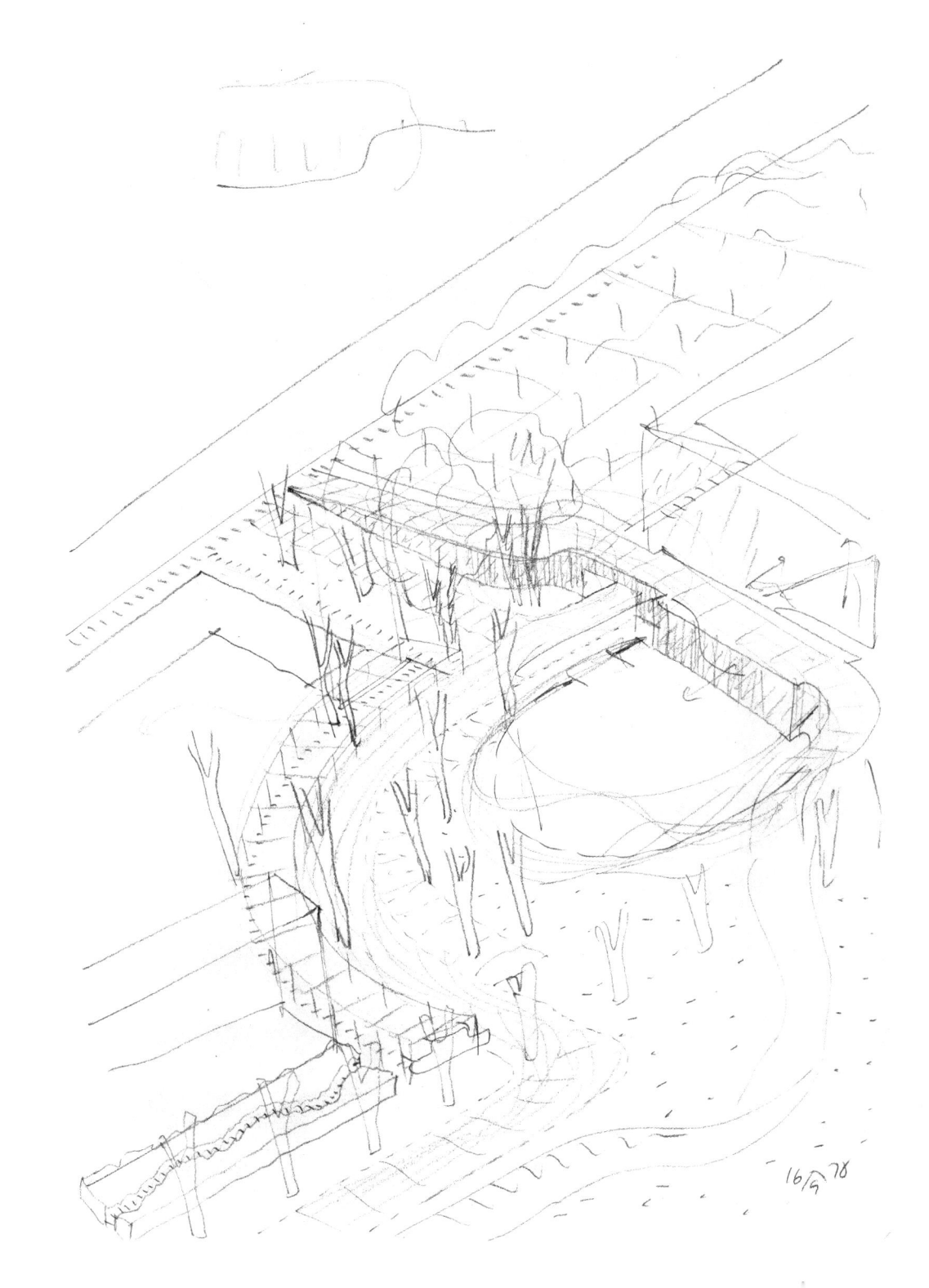

Three projects in conversation
Gentofte Library, 1978

Mødesalen er udformet med et stort sidelys mod øst.
På de tilbagetrukne vægge på de to af rummets sider er der gode betingelser
for at supplere udstillingsrummets ophængningsmuligheder, og ved større
udstillinger, vil sideslyset kunne bidrage til større variationer i udstillingens
opbygning.
Mødesalen har direkte adgang til cafeen via en lille tilbagetrukket niche med
magelige siddepladser og udsigt til parken.

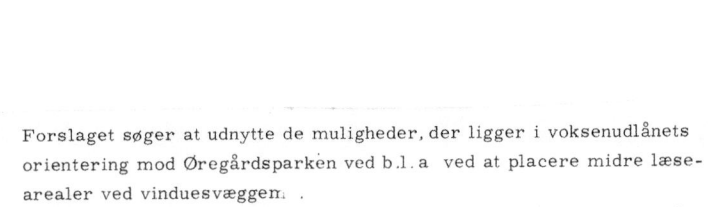

Forslaget søger at udnytte de muligheder, der ligger i voksenudlånets
orientering mod Øregårdsparken ved b.l.a ved at placere midre læse-
arealer ved vinduesvæggen.
Det nordvestlige hjørne af bygningen ligger særlig gunstigt m.h.t. både
sol og udsigt. (p.g.a. den særlige udformning af taget med ovenlys, vil
der være sol i rummet allerede fra kl 12). Forslaget placerer en større
læsegruppe på dette sted, der samtidig er tyngdepunktet i voksenudlånet.
Opstillingen af reoler i voksenudlånet indebærer iøvrigt, at man hele
tiden kan opfatte udsigten til parken i små glimt.

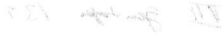

MoFA

MoFA

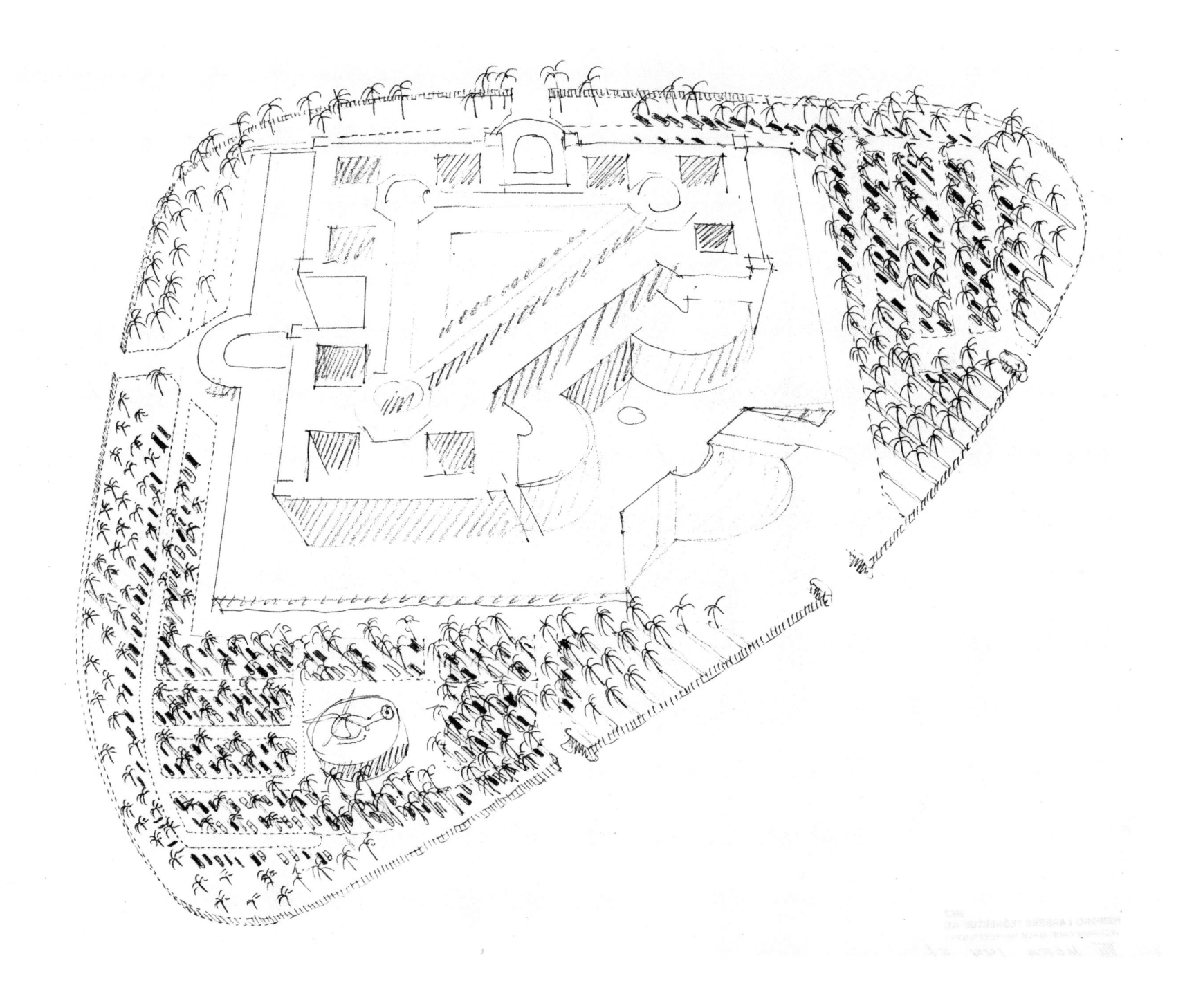

The Ministry of Foreign Affairs in Riyadh (MoFA), Saudi Arabia, is Henning Larsen's masterpiece. In *Architectural Review* (no. 1061, July 1985), Chris Abel wrote that the structure was probably a 'turning point in the architecture of the twentieth century'. It combines modern and historical, Western and Islamic architecture in a manner that had not been seen before, and it contains a range of sensory experiences far beyond those of a normal office building.

The competition was held in 1980, in two stages, while the construction happened between 1982 and 1984. During the four-year process Henning Larsen made several hundred sketches featuring different purposes. There are sketches from the dialogue at the drafting boards and analytical sketches and drawings of Islamic architecture, in Saudi Arabia and across the Islamic world, from Morocco to Bangladesh. There are drawings made for descriptions and presentation boards, and there are architectural fantasies rhapsodizing on various aspects of the project.

The sketches range from the big overall plan to lighting details, and there is literally not a corner of the building Henning Larsen didn't consider and discuss with the many people involved with the project design. It is also very clear that Henning Larsen used drawings to prepare for conversations with the client. Some were made at the office in Copenhagen, probably while going through details before a trip to Saudi Arabia; others were made on the plane or at the hotel.

In this project, principles established and tested in the University of Trondheim project, in the school in Høje-Taastrup and in the Gentofte Library project meet with ideas that were never realized, for instance in a project for a courthouse and housing in Berlin. The large, complex structure requires a contemporary approach, but the project combines the overall organizational concept of streets and squares as in Trondheim with a formal boost of energy as in Høje-Taastrup, informed by a thorough study of Islamic architecture.

Henning Larsen typically drew certain main motifs from these projects over and again. There are motifs specific not just to the projects but also to spaces that had been with him for his entire life, such as the panopticon and the monumental staircase. During his studies of Islamic architecture, Larsen developed a new element: the hidden tower. In Riyadh it functions as a meeting place in the corners of the triangular plan, and it is found again in several later projects, not least the Business School in Frederiksberg.

Even though the project for the Foreign Ministry in Riyadh evolved from ideas already present at the Henning Larsen Office, it is notable that the design is more of a mass from which parts are extracted than it is a structure composed of elements. It is clear from the remaining sketches that Larsen was preoccupied with this, for him, new way of thinking about space, and he experimented with the forms that arose from this method. Perhaps because it is a transitional stage between the two ways of shaping architecture, the inner spaces are often drawn as objects, where the tower is one example among others.

Within the modern tradition that Henning Larsen was grounded in, mainly with inspiration from Le Corbusier but including roots in Kay Fisker's 'Danish Tradition', cities and buildings were imagined as things that were combined from different elements. The elements could be as small as bricks or as big as cathedrals, but they were clearly delimited as objects each with their own form and identity, even though the cathedral is obviously made of many stones. This is how computer programs for construction are designed to work today.

But there has long been a parallel tradition that has perhaps grown out of the way one experiences the historical centre of Rome today: as a series of spaces that are carved out of a dense mass. One might recognize this way of thinking from the Danish architect C.F. Hansen, who rebuilt Copenhagen after the great fires and the bombardment in 1807. Or think of the Englishman John Soane, who transformed and built the Bank of England around the same time.

Obviously, this type of architecture is built from elements like bricks and windows just like the other type. But in the imagination and development process of the architect, all the parts must service the whole, the spaces and their relations.

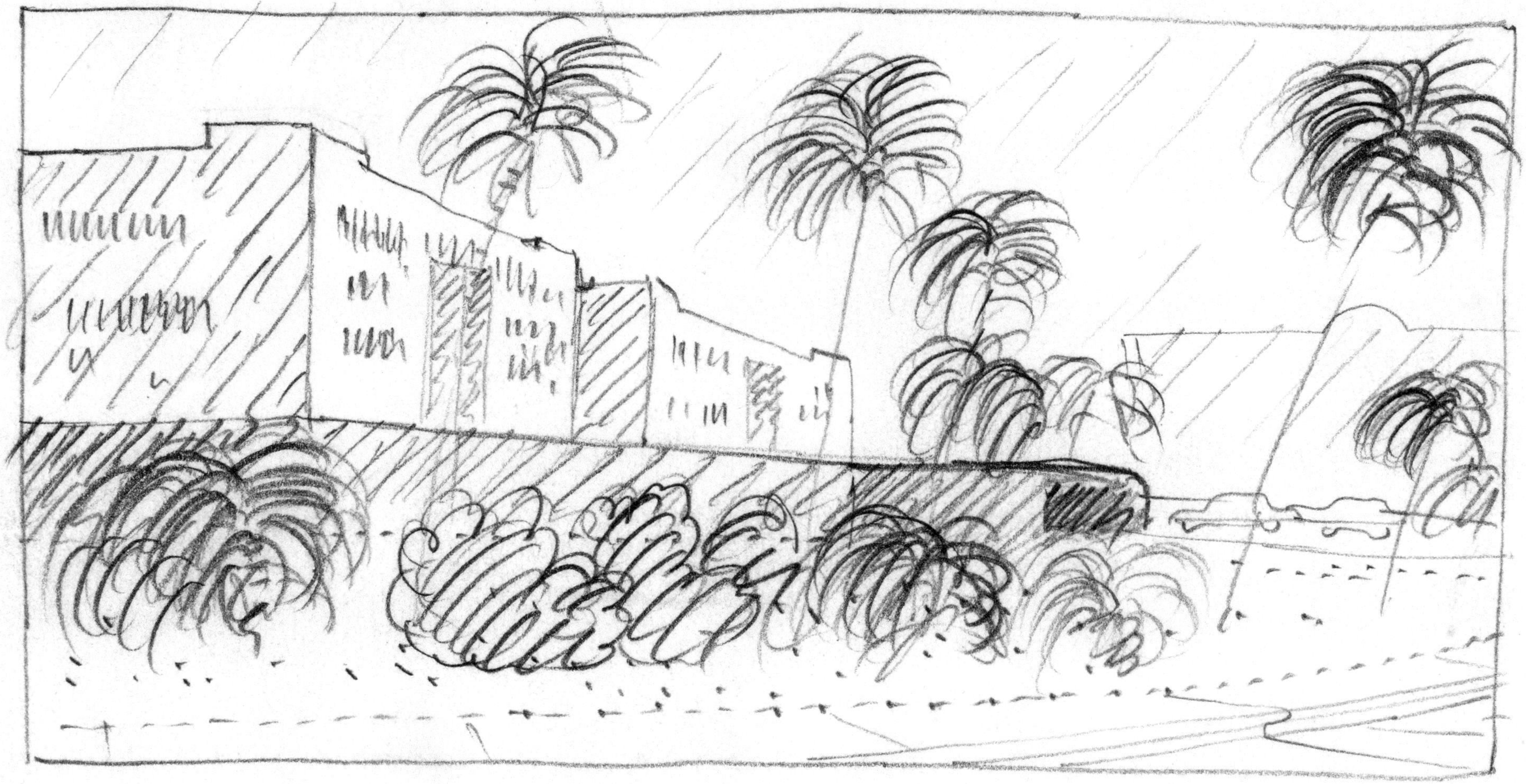

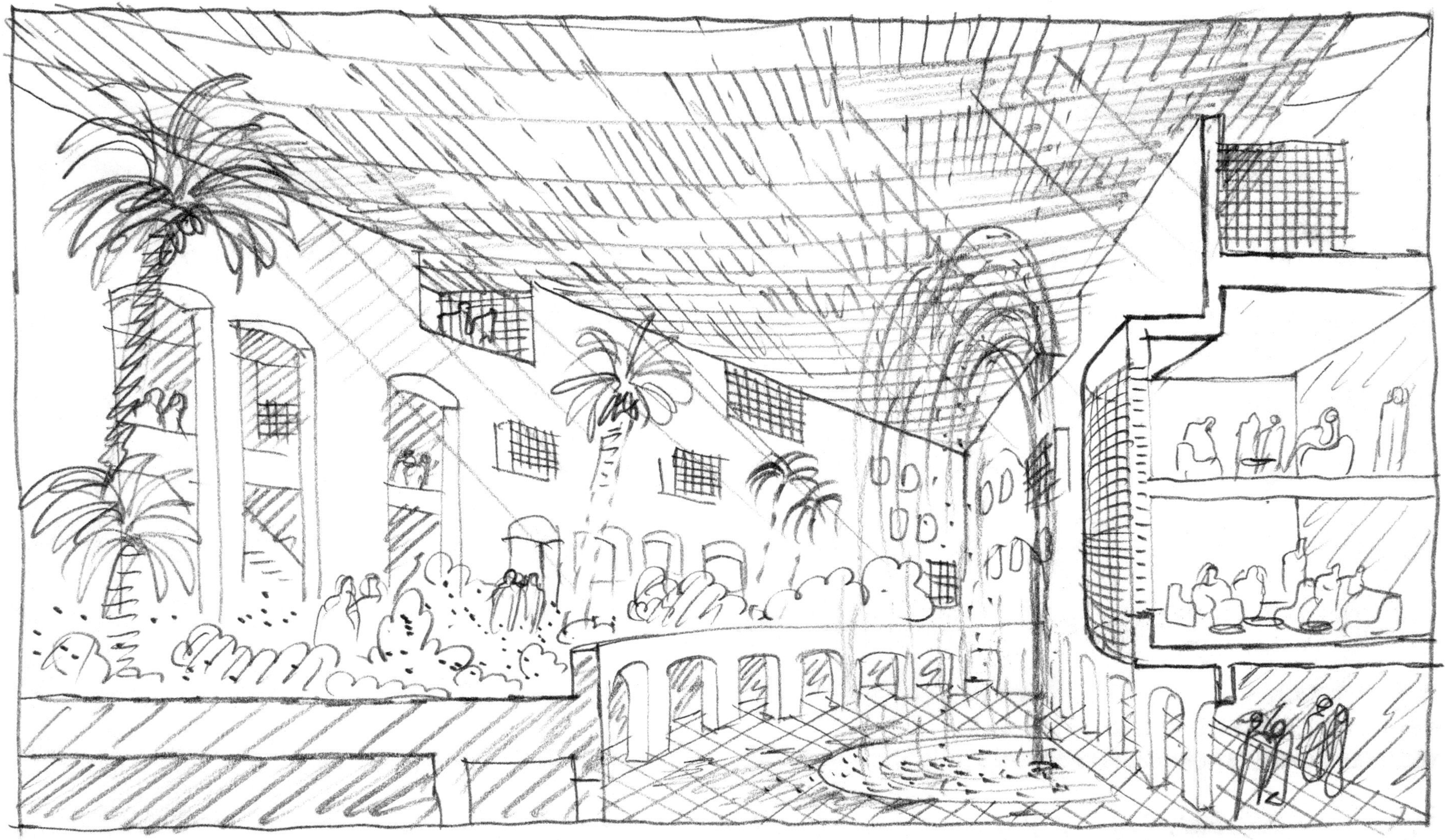

MoFA 100

101

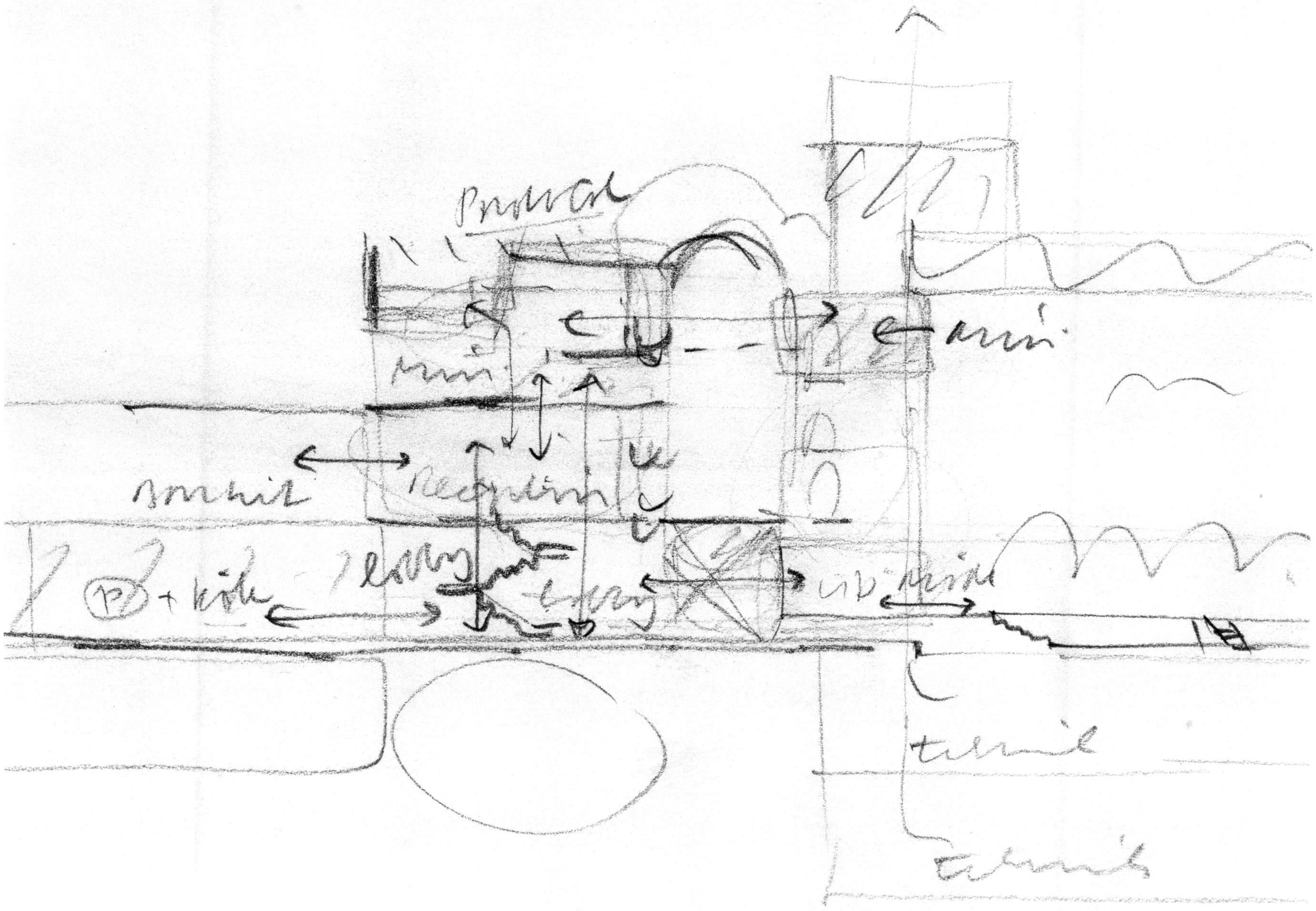

a b c d

02

MoFA

105

MoFA 106

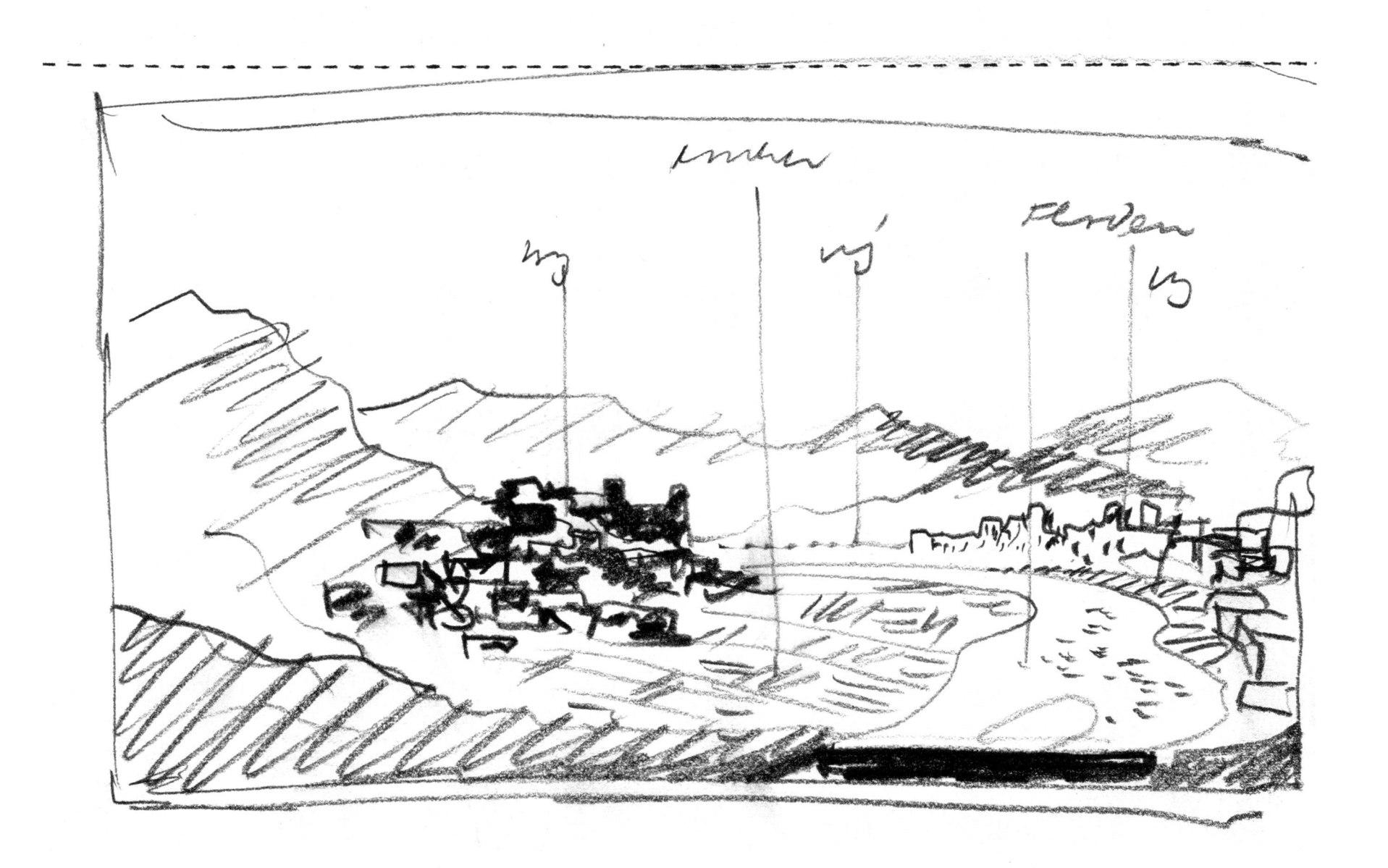

RABAT

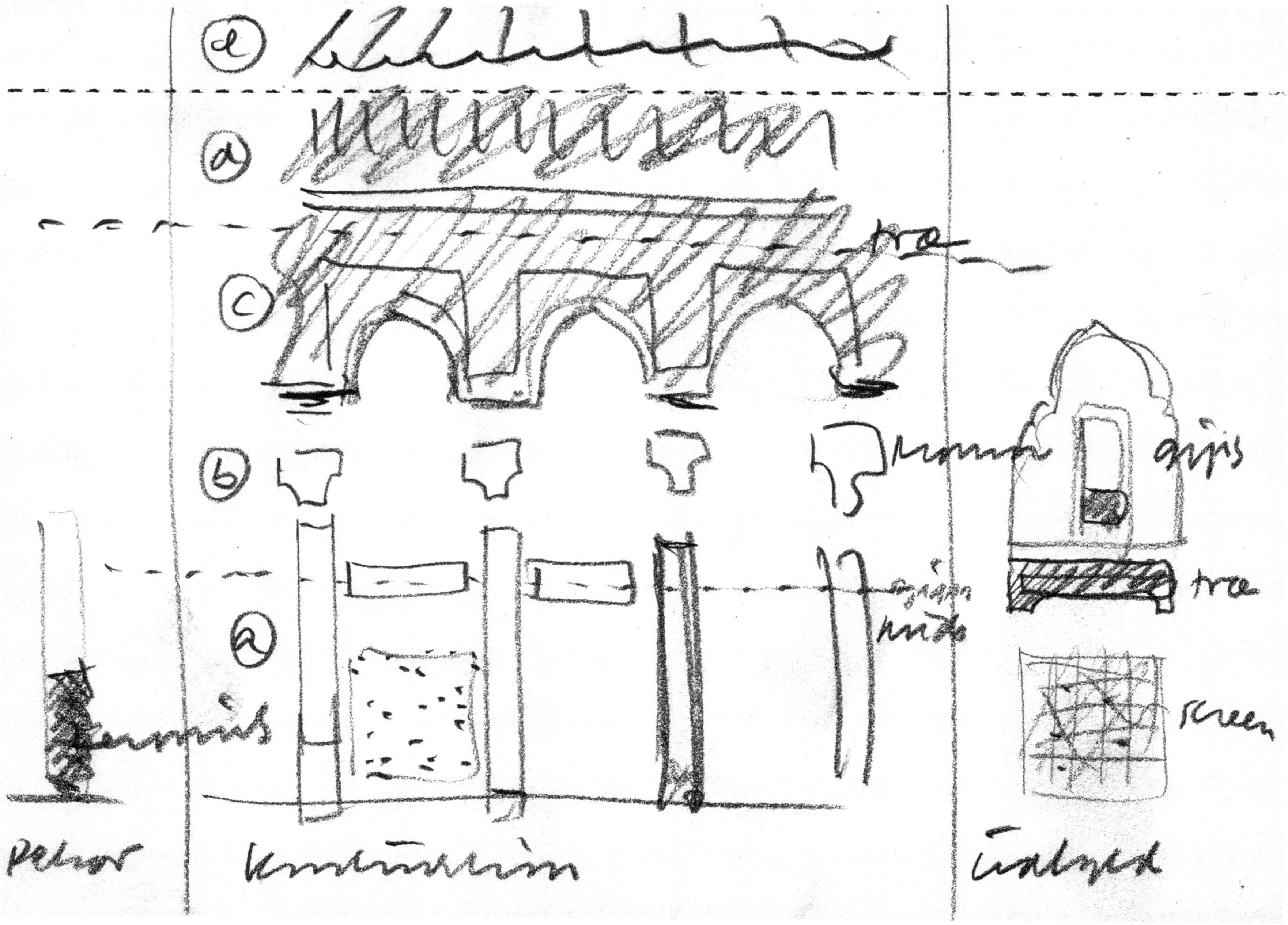
tra
gips
tra
screen

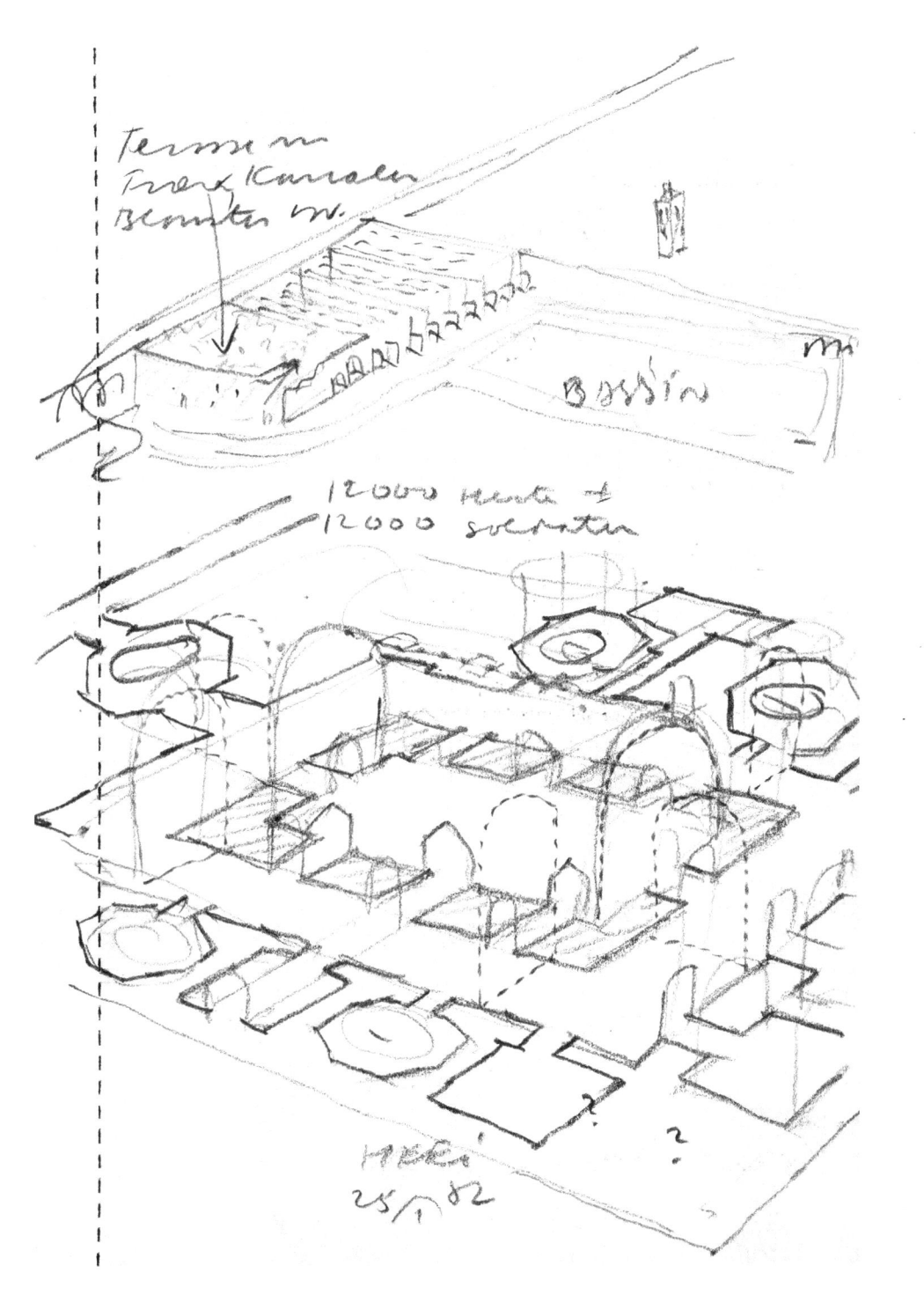

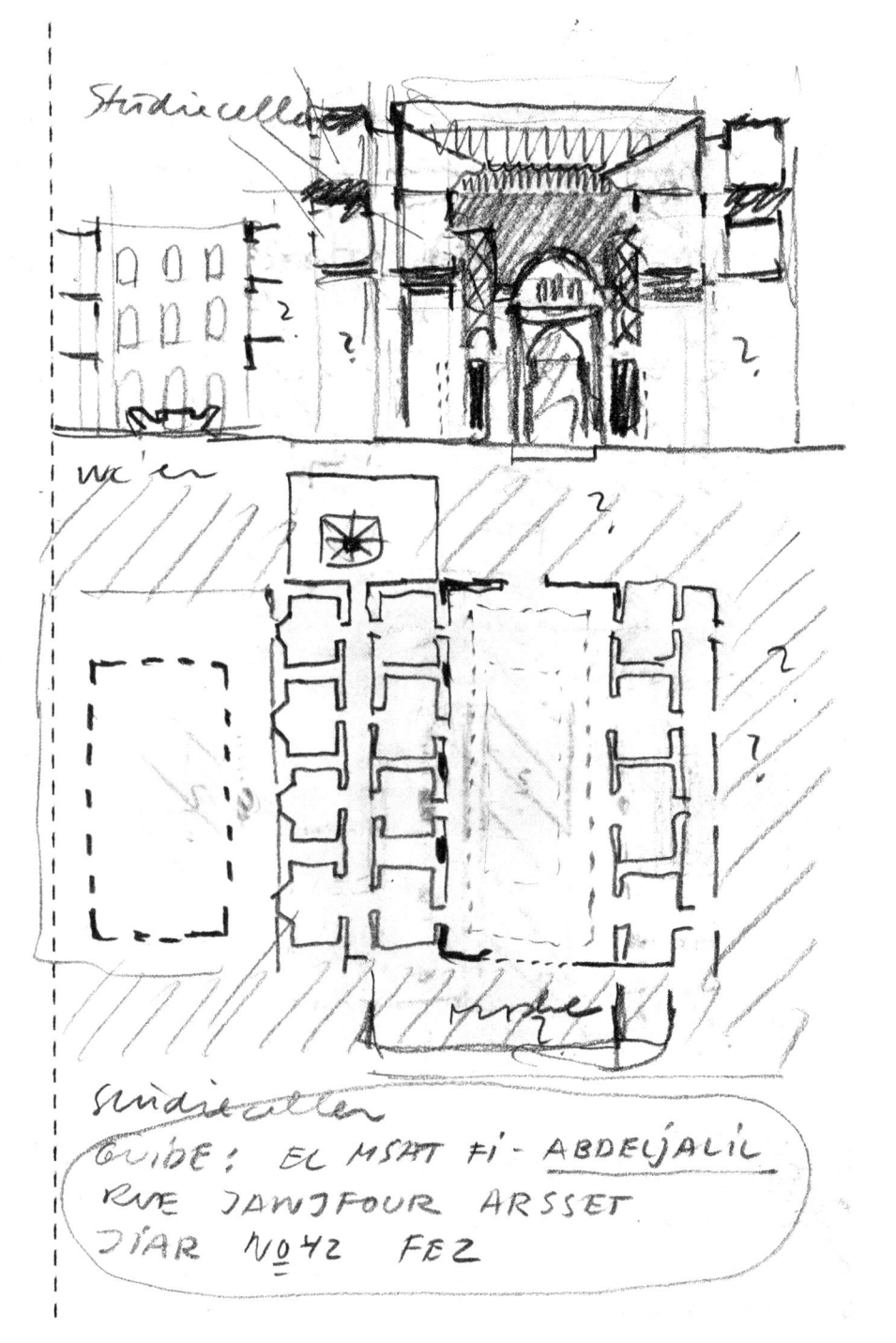

GUIDE: EL MSAT FI-ABDELJALIL
RUE JAWJFOUR ARSSET
DIAR N° 42 FEZ

MoFA

111

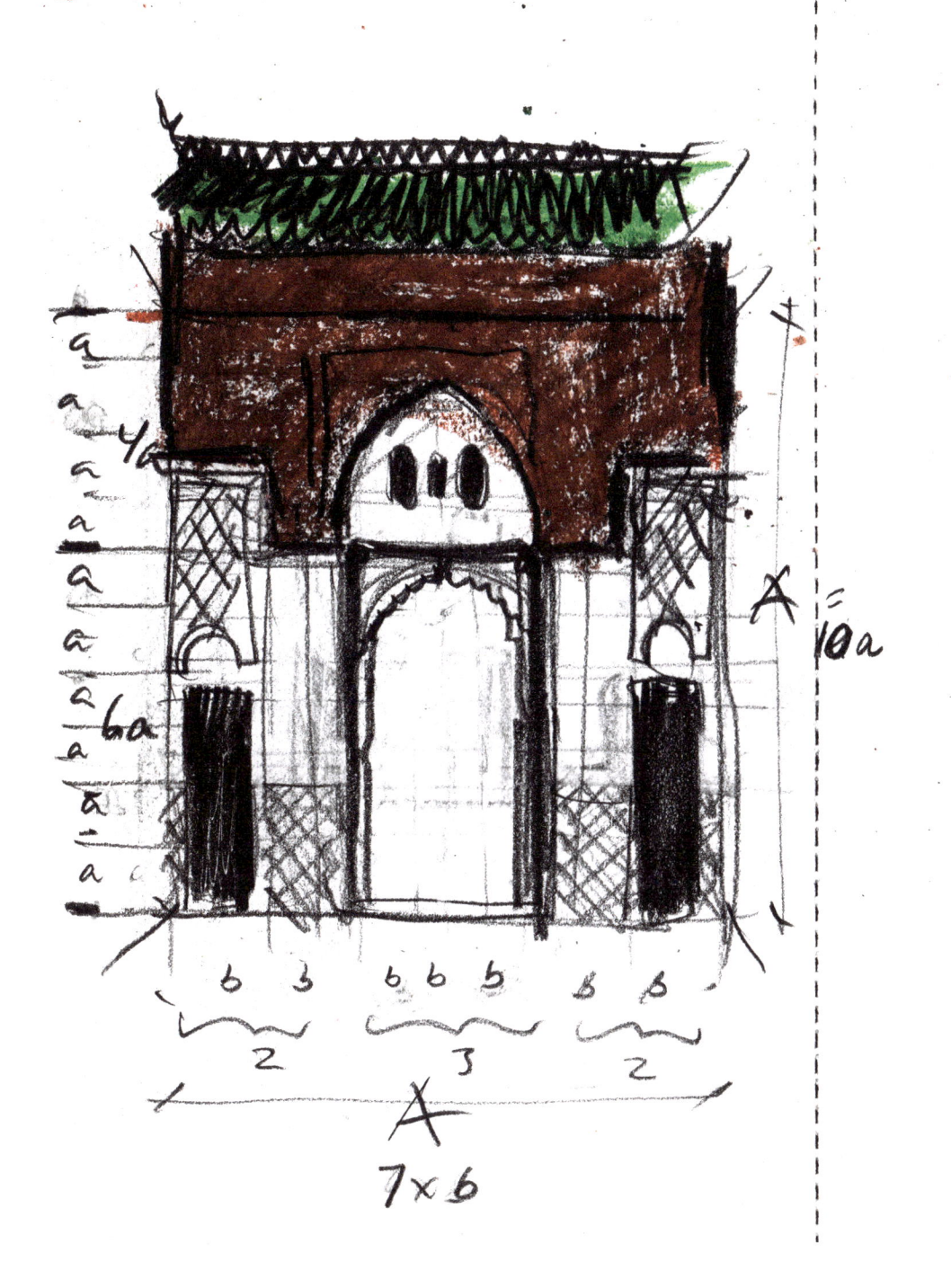

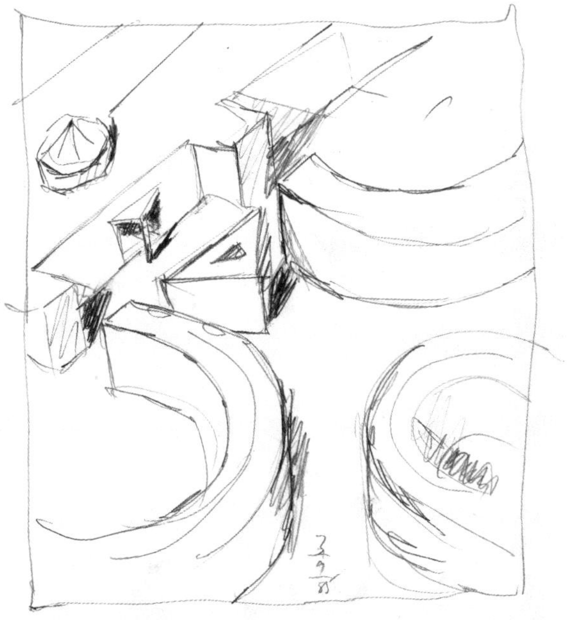

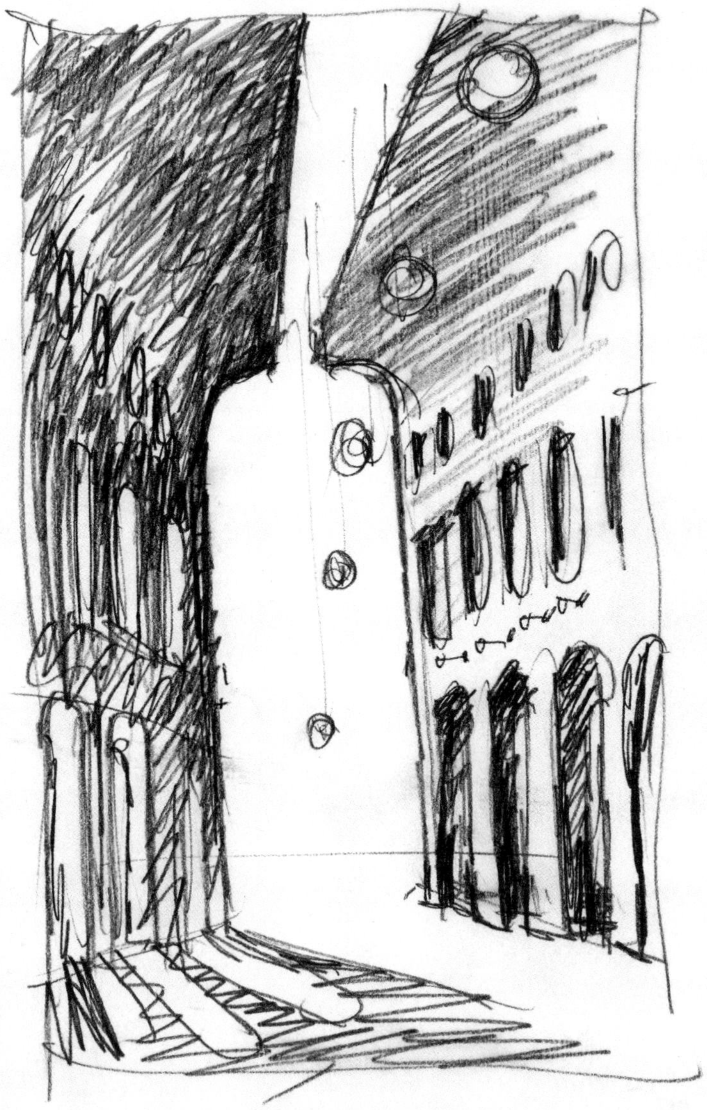

MoFA

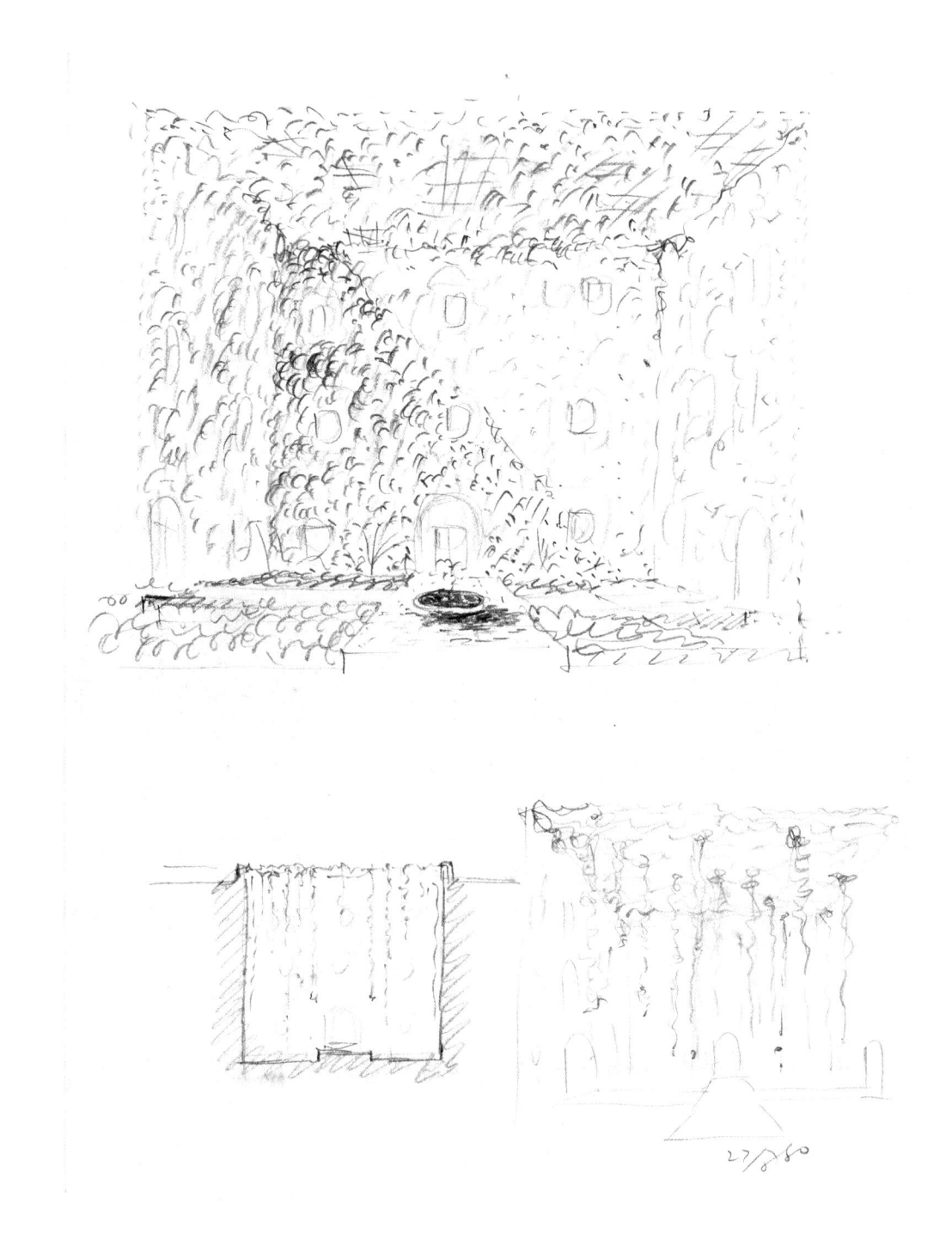

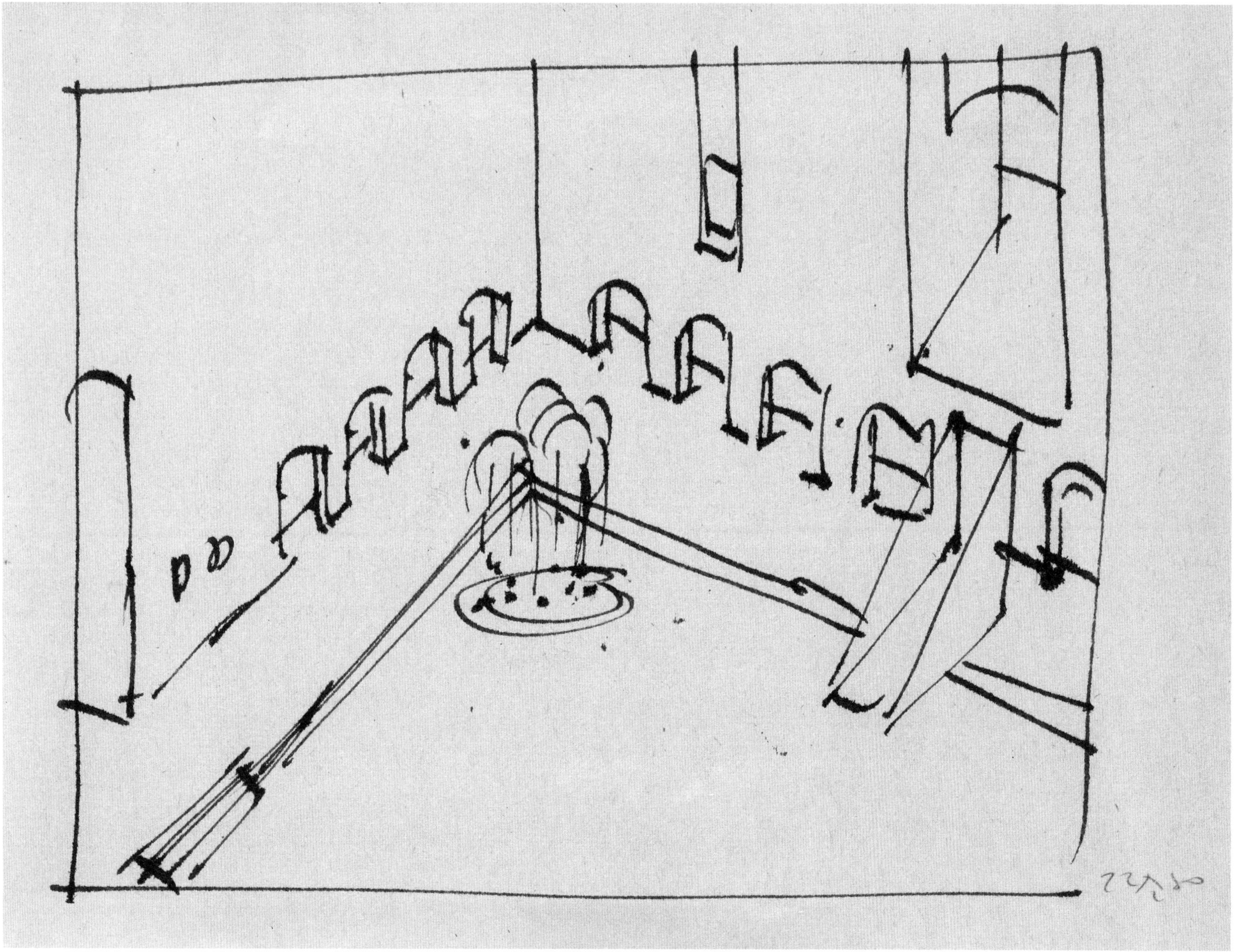

115

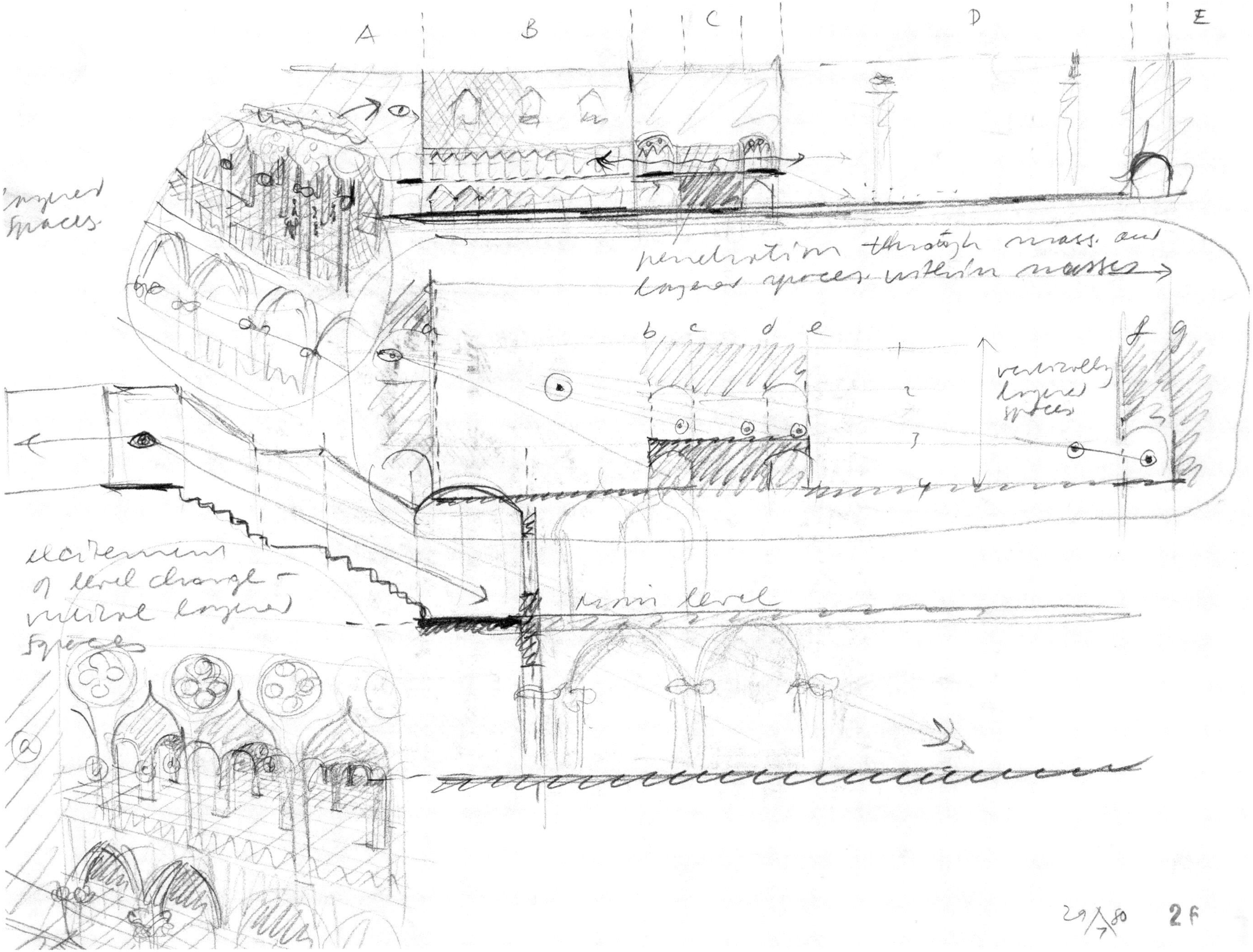
A
B
C
D
E
layered spaces
penetration through mass and layered spaces within masses
b c d e
f g
vertically layered spaces
main level
29/7/80
2F

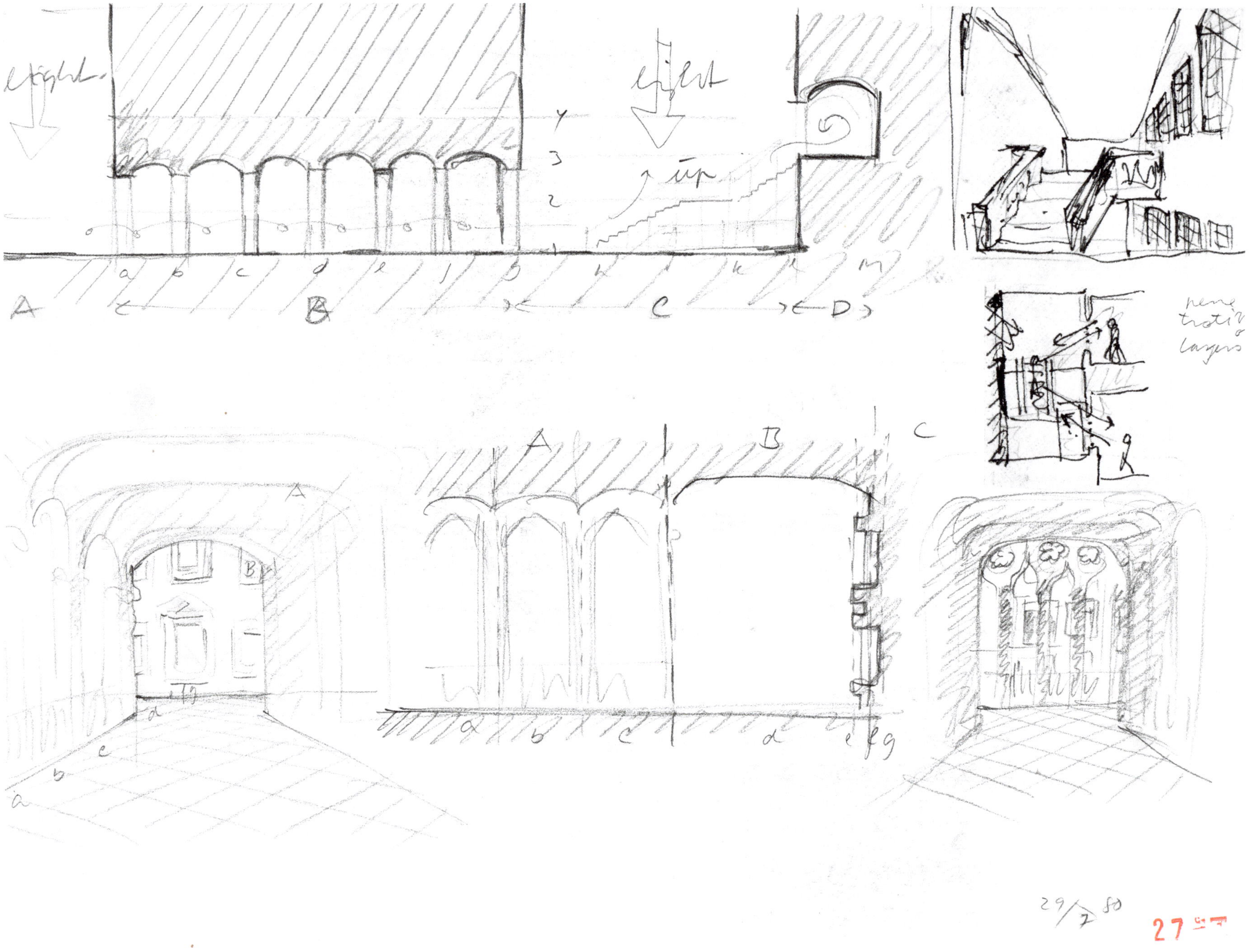
light
light
up
A
B
C
D
29/2 80
27

'Layered spaces' is another motif that turns up in the context of the Foreign Ministry and then becomes a common theme in Henning Larsen's work. In this case, there is a well-defined moment of inspiration: during the work on the second round of the competition for the Ministry, Henning Larsen visited the first Architecture Biennale in Venice. While there, he made analytical sketches of the Doge Palace, emphasizing the layered spaces.

At his hotel room, he made a drawing of one of the corner towers for the Riyadh project, translating the inspiration from the Doge Palace into the proposal. Given that the Venetian architecture of the late Middle Ages was inspired by Islamic architecture, Henning Larsen draws a full circle of inspiration through the ages and across borders.

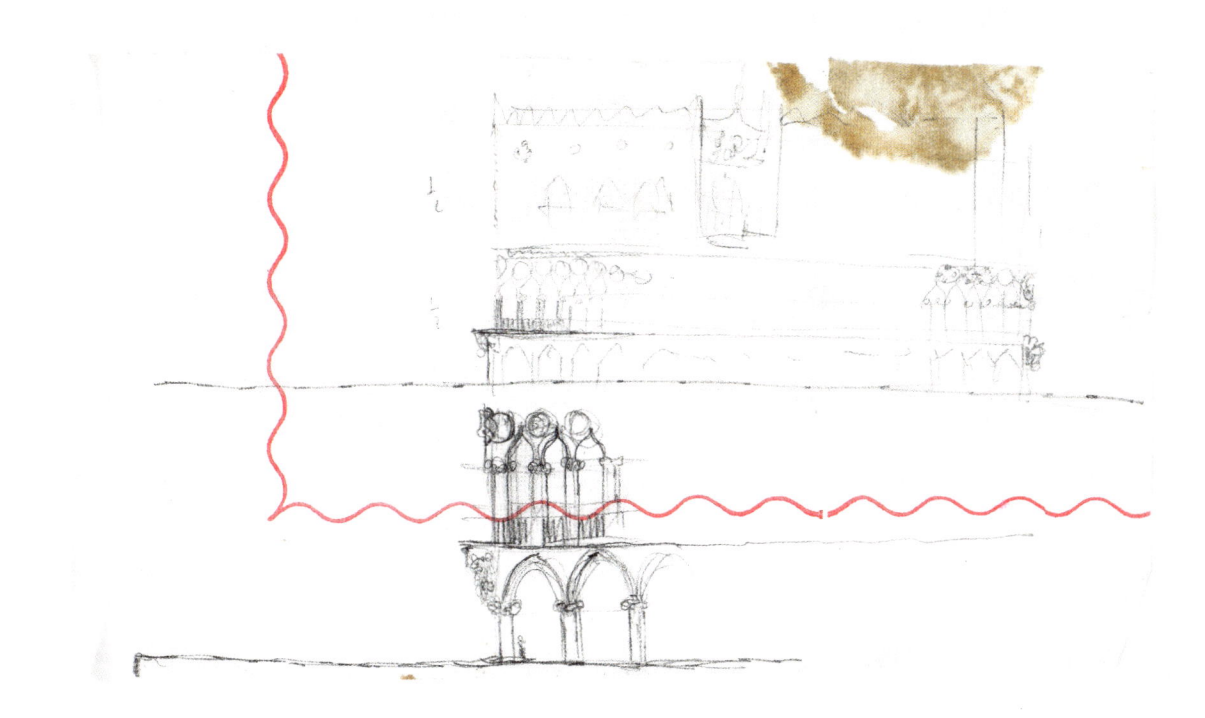

HLT
HENNING LARSENS TEGNESTUE A/S
VESTERBROGADE 76 • DK 1620 KØBENHAVN V
Shade
Mass
Light
Space
Mass
Layered spaces
modulates movement
29/7 80

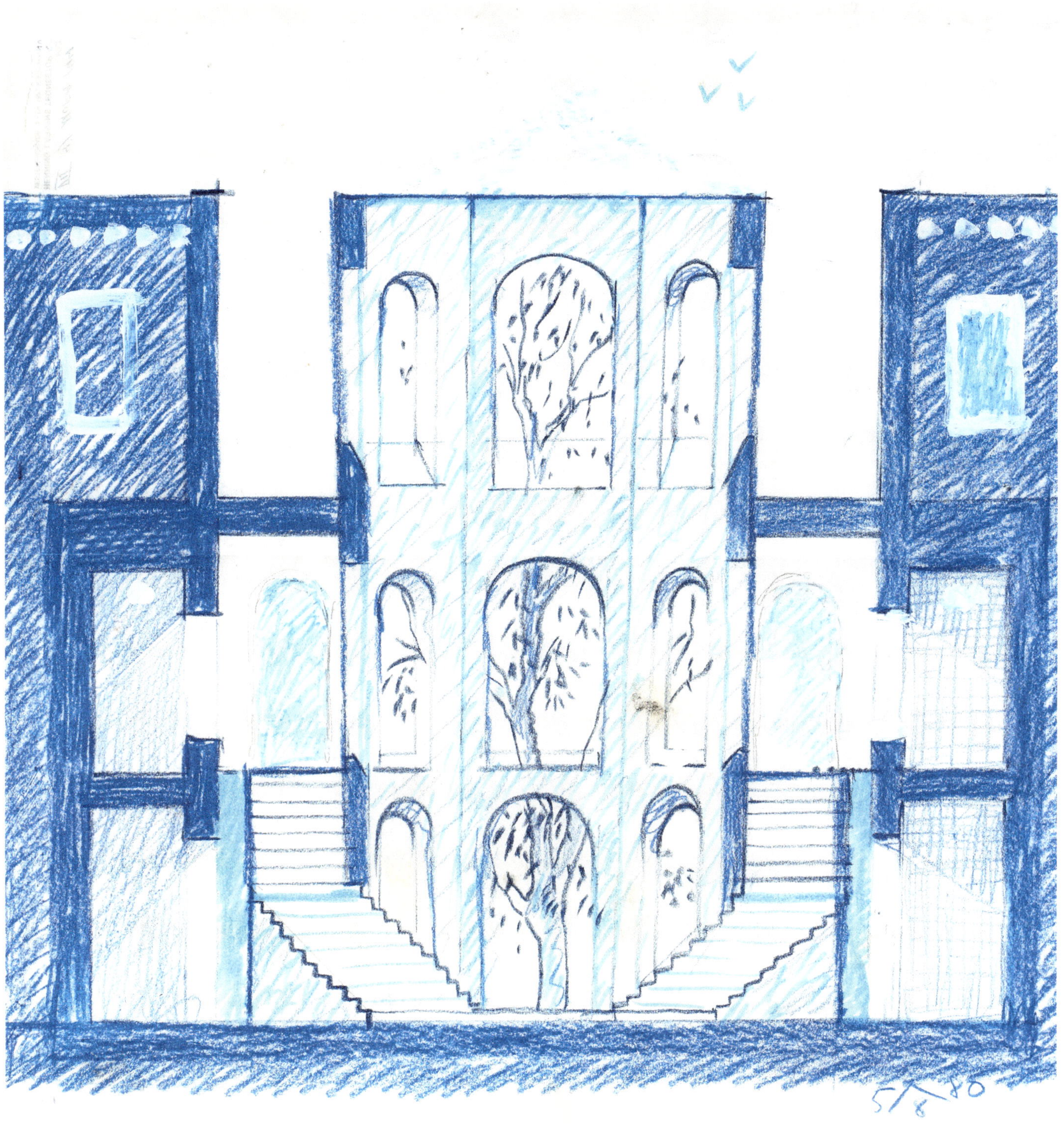
5/8 80

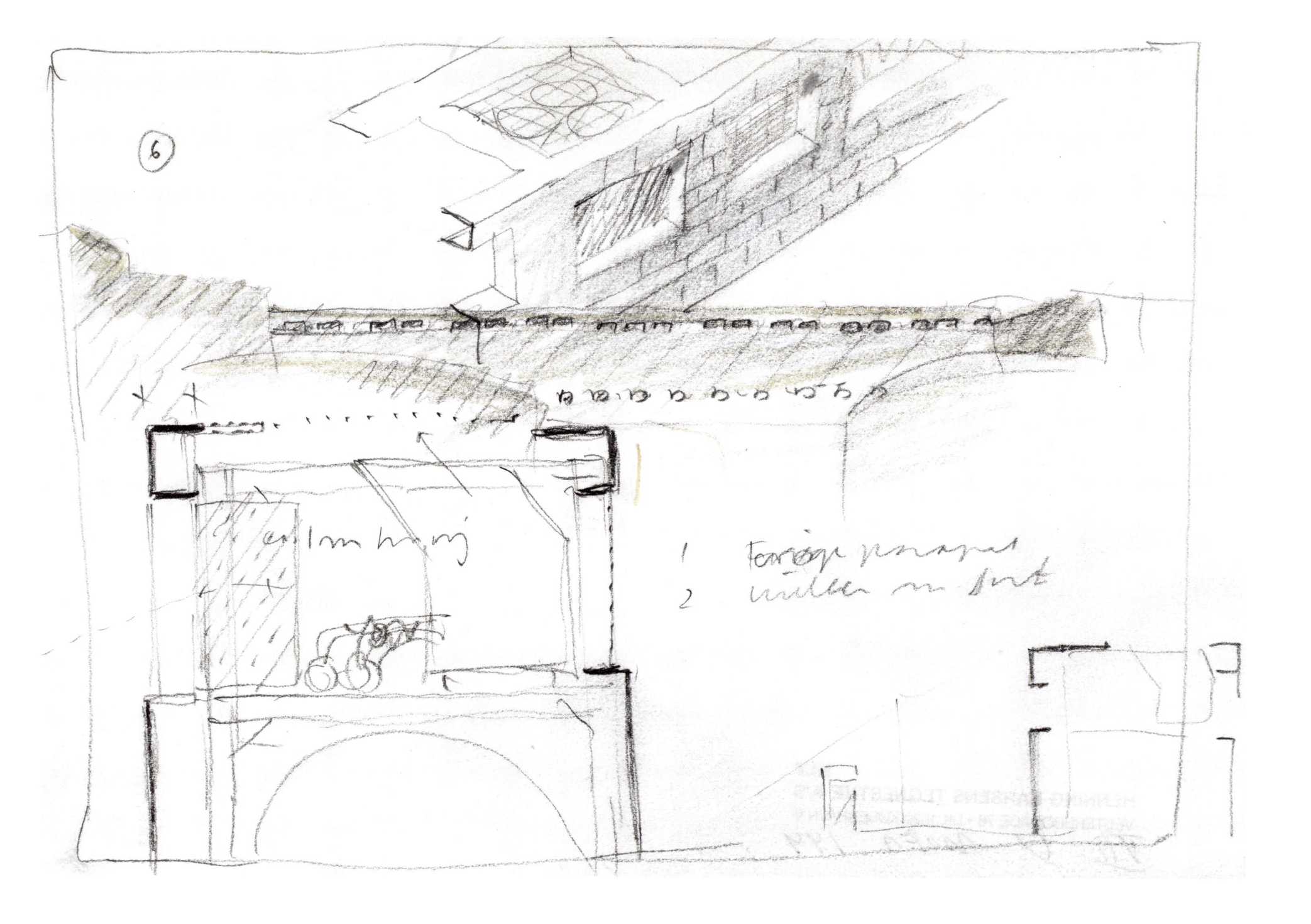

MoFA

The concept of layered spaces reappears in the handling of daylight.

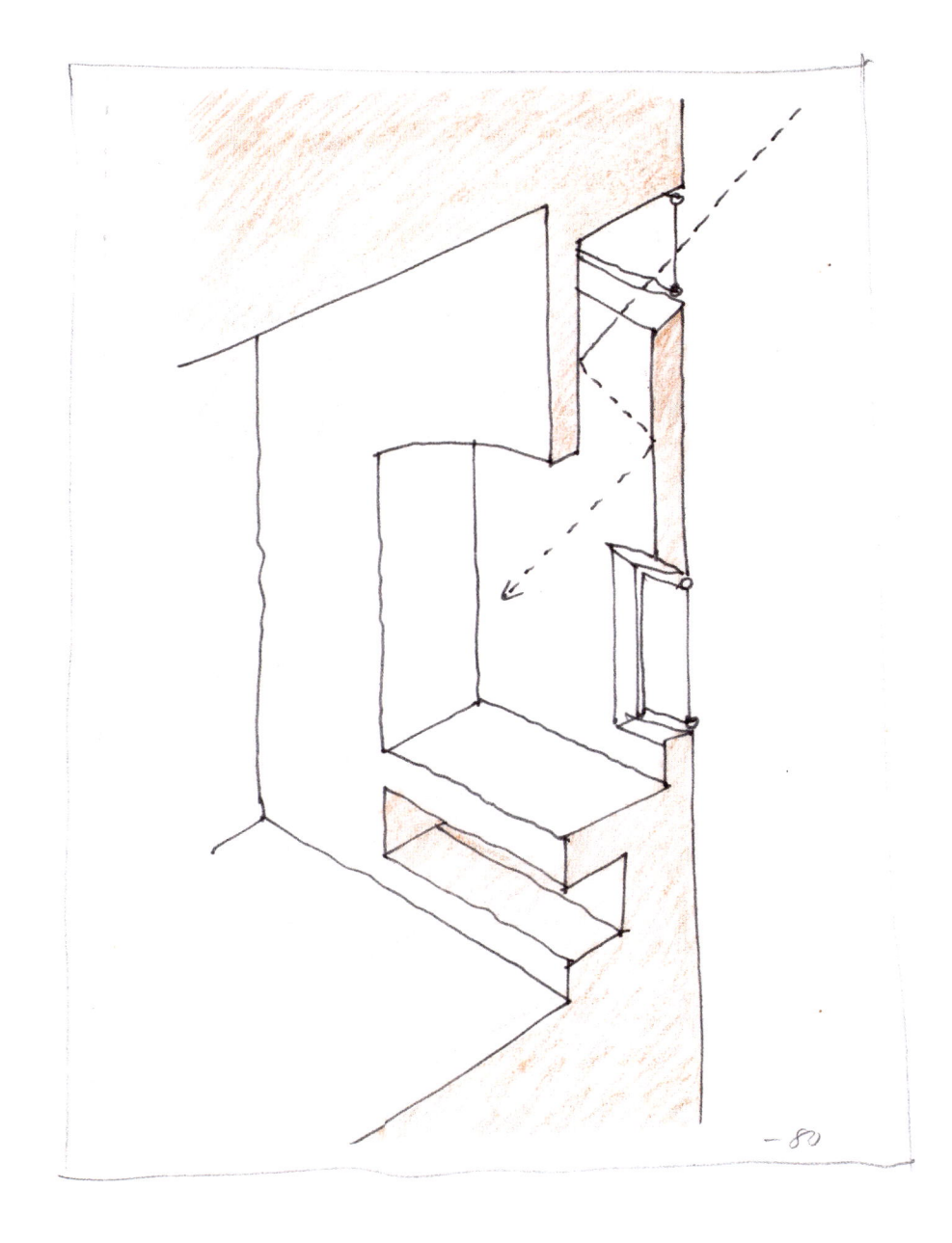

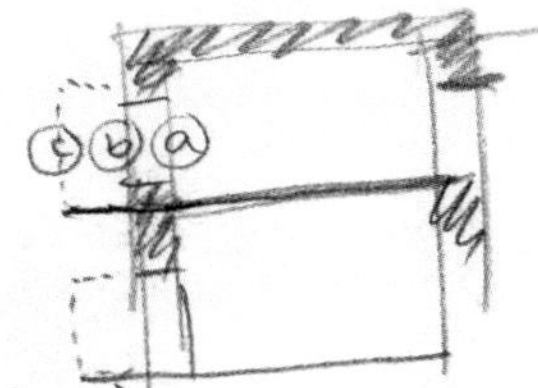

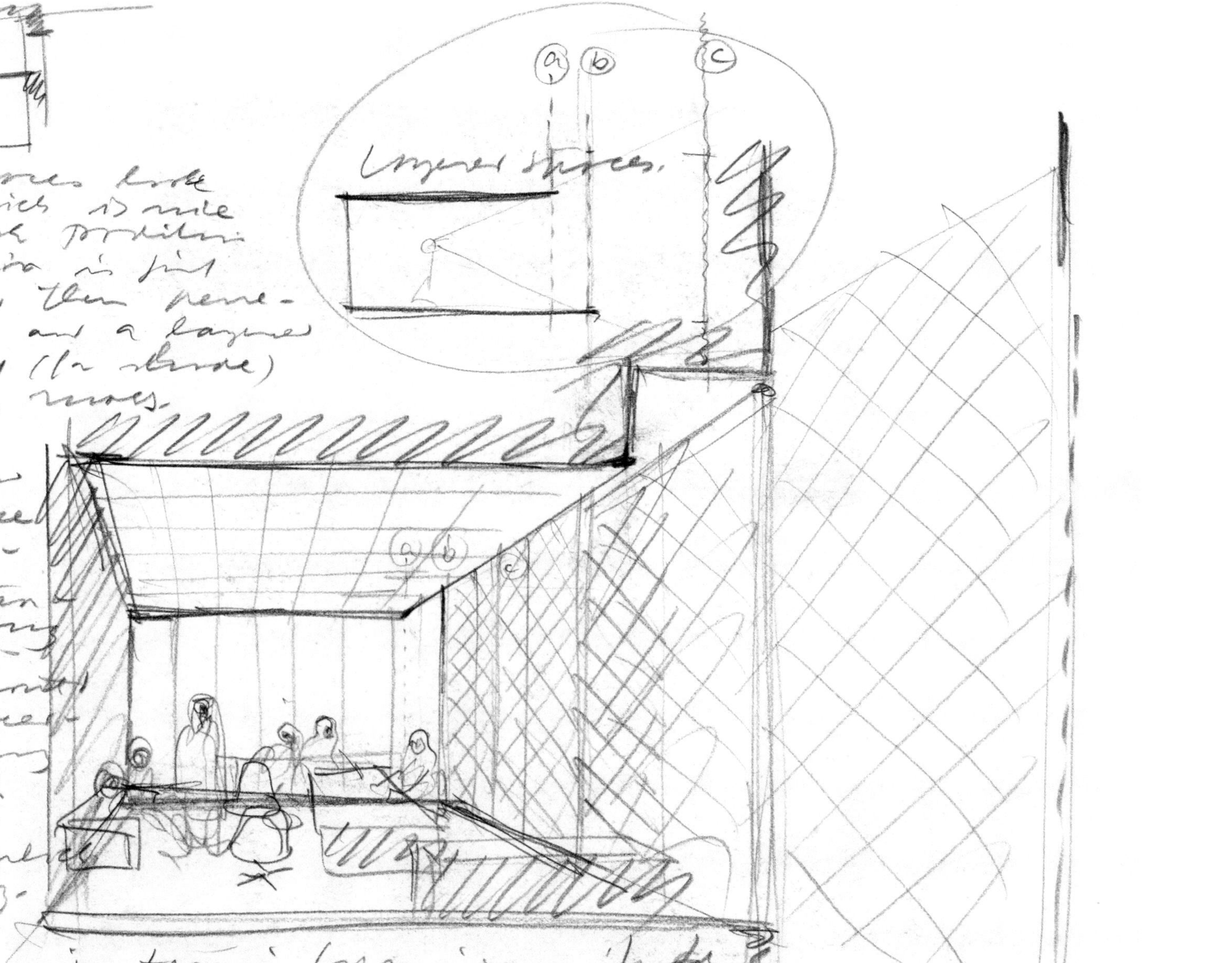

MoFA

MoFA

127

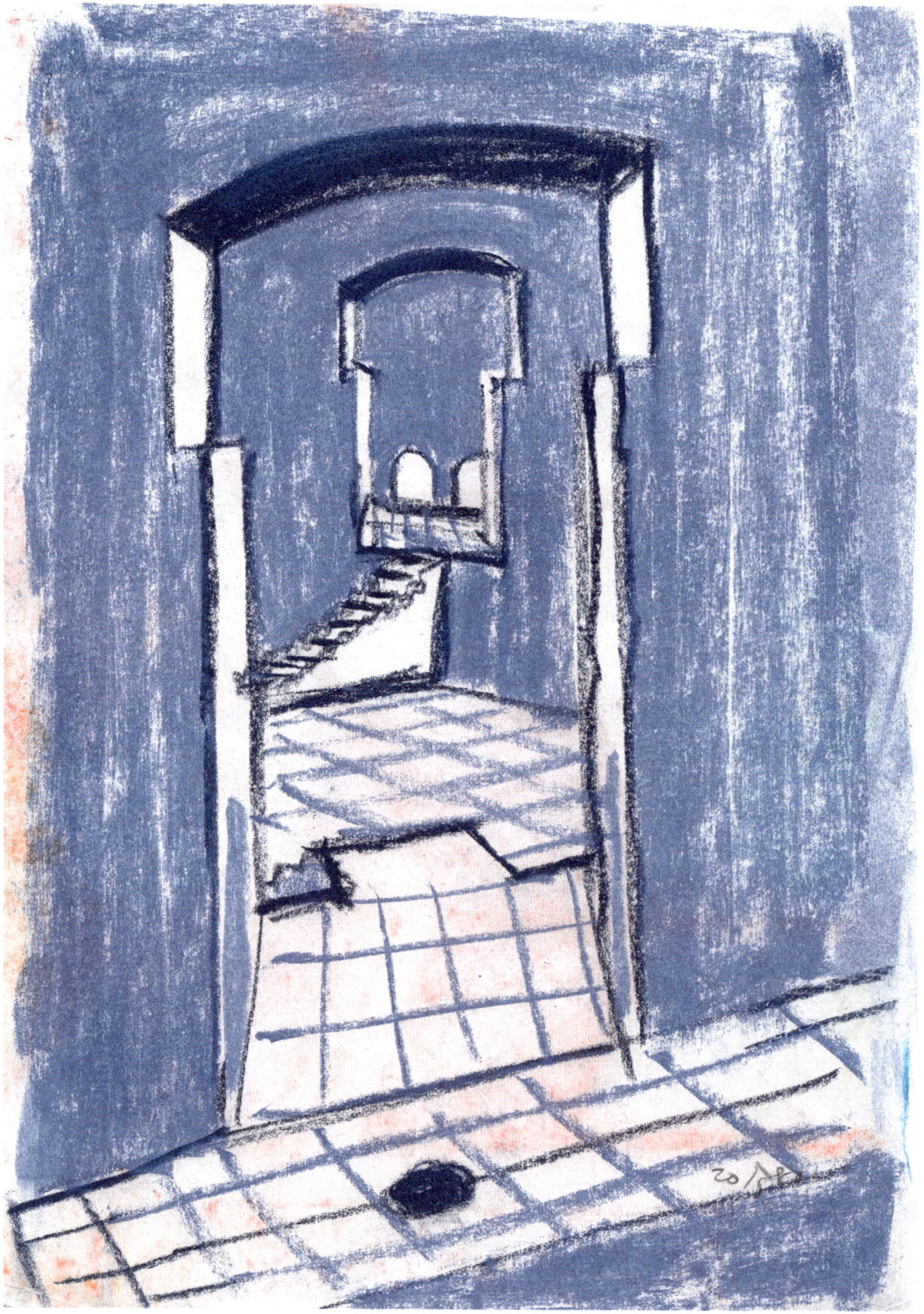

While the project was developed and worked through at the office, Henning Larsen also worked with a series of pastel drawings that were more of an artistic exploration of the motifs and inspirational elements from the project. Some became part of the representation of the project on boards, in descriptions and in journals, but others had no purpose beyond the artistic. Throughout his life, Henning Larsen was preoccupied with contemporary art, and he was clearly inspired by graphic art and painting in his drawings. Among the drawings from the Riyadh period is this sketch in strong colours that seems inspired by David Hockney, both in colour, the angle of the view and the framing.

MoFA

Copenhagen Business School and Dalgas Have

Copenhagen Business School
and Dalgas Have

The Business School and Dalgas Have (Dalgas Gardens) were two large continuous projects in Frederiksberg, a district of Copenhagen. Here many of the motifs from the Ministry of Foreign Affairs were reused and developed further, for instance the understanding of the buildings as masses, the staircases, the layered spaces and the inner towers.

Selected motifs are repeatedly redrawn, and the artistic development of the sketch in itself is continued.

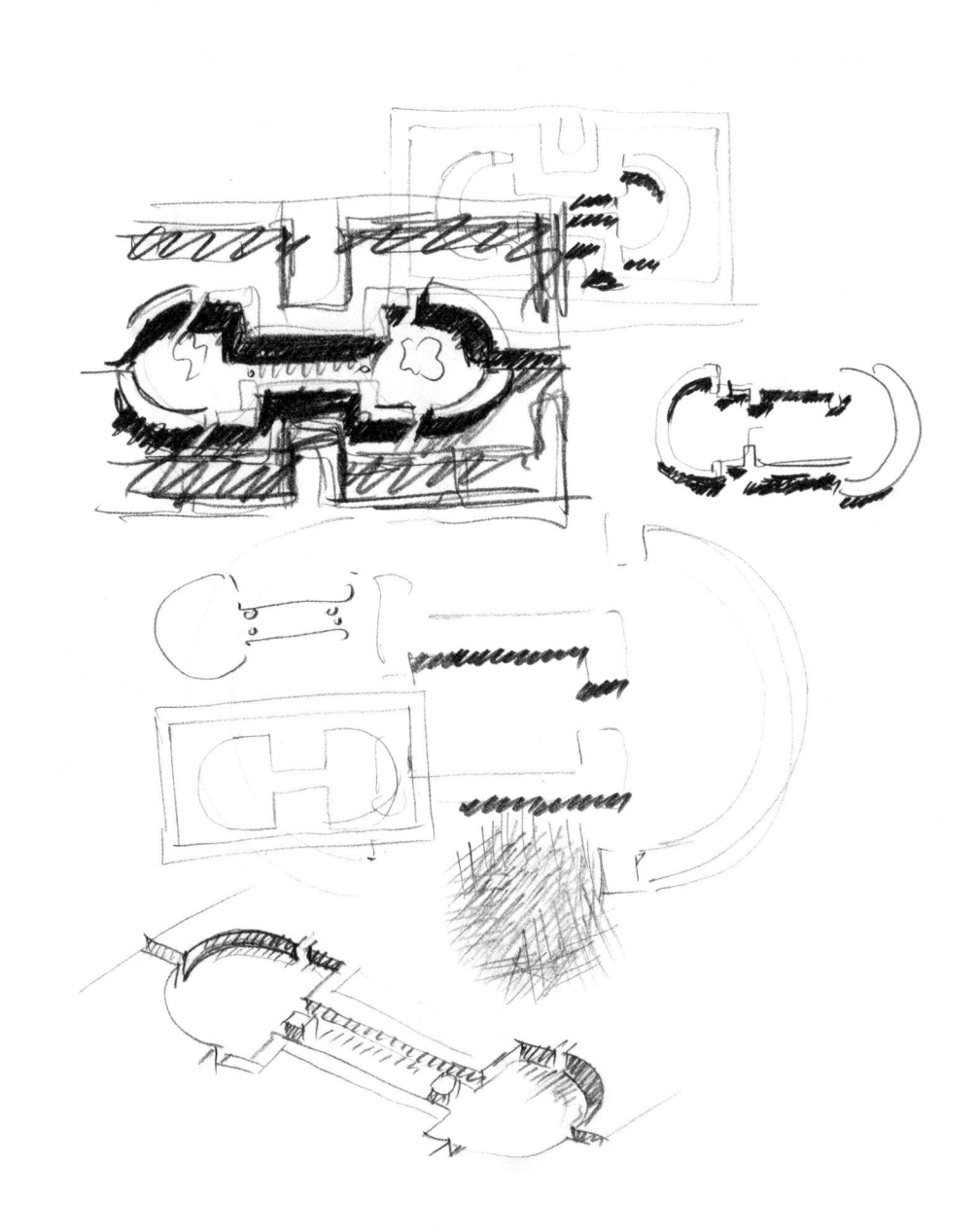

Copenhagen Business School
and Dalgas Have

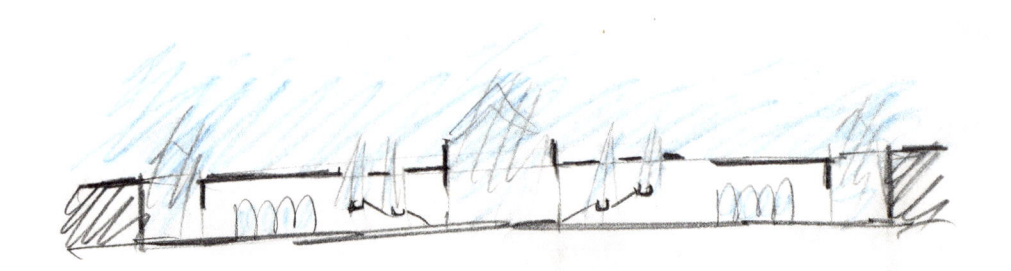

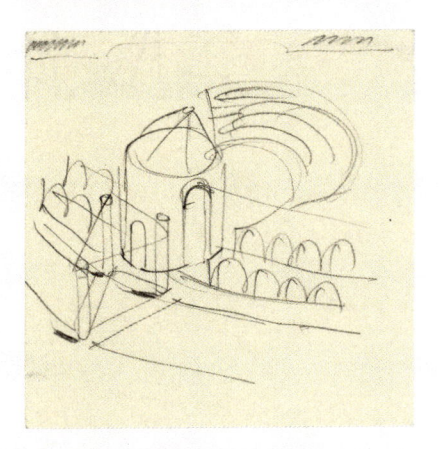

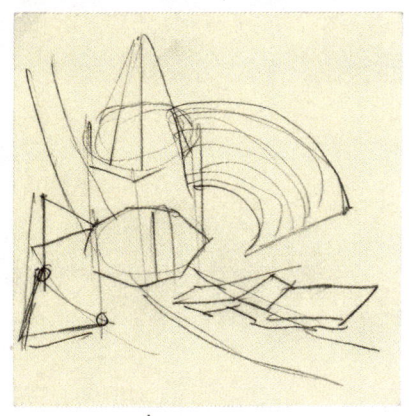

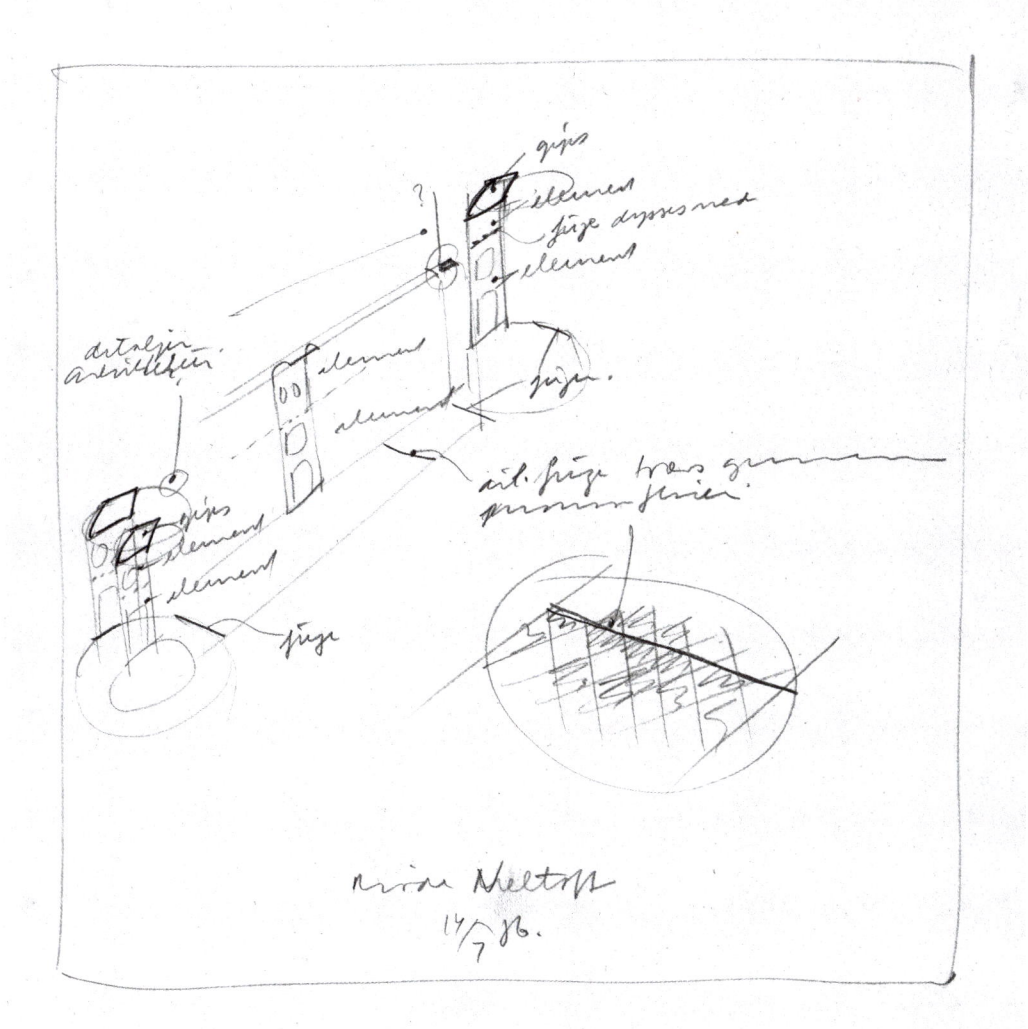

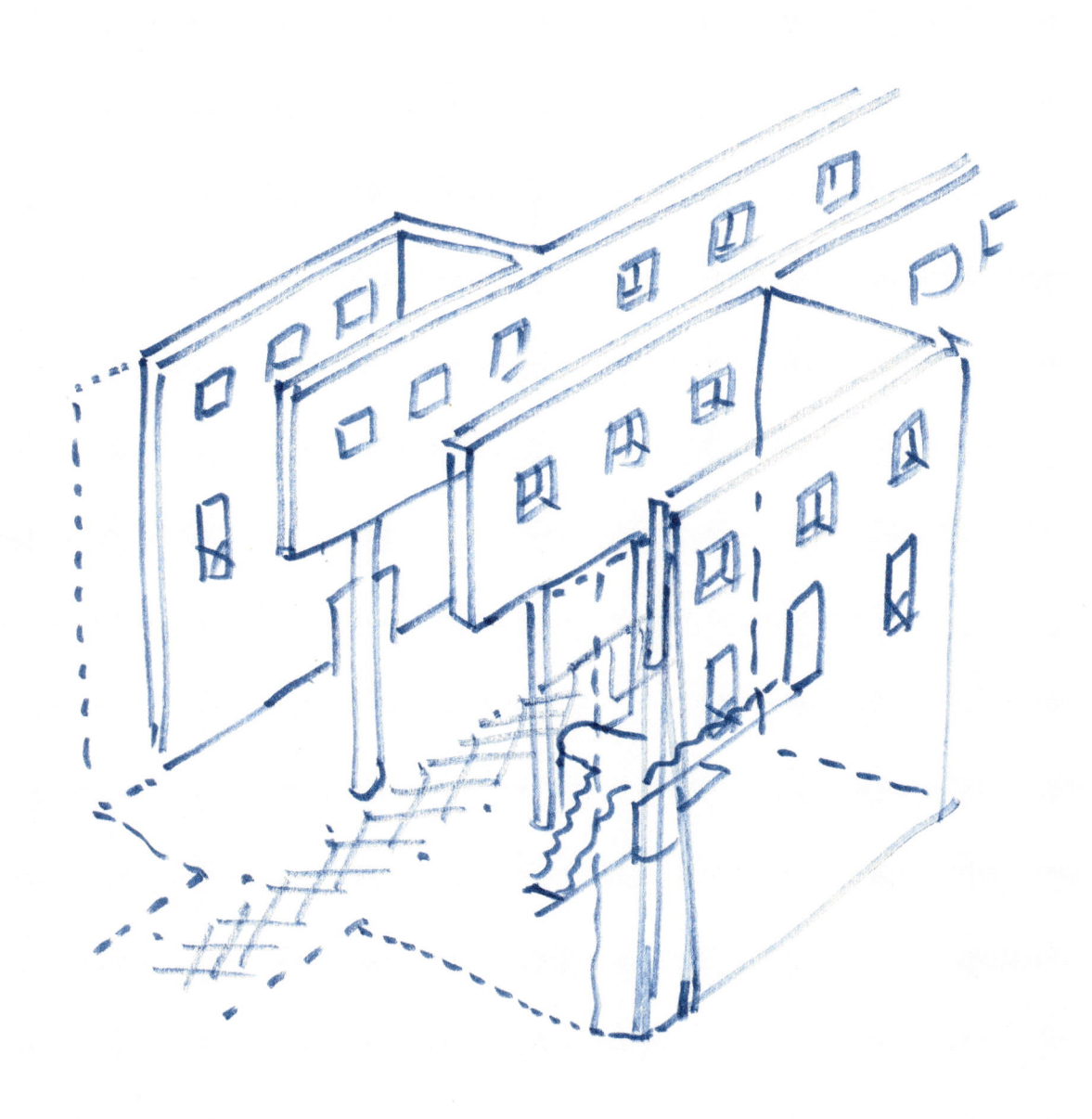

Copenhagen Business School
and Dalgas Have

bibliotek

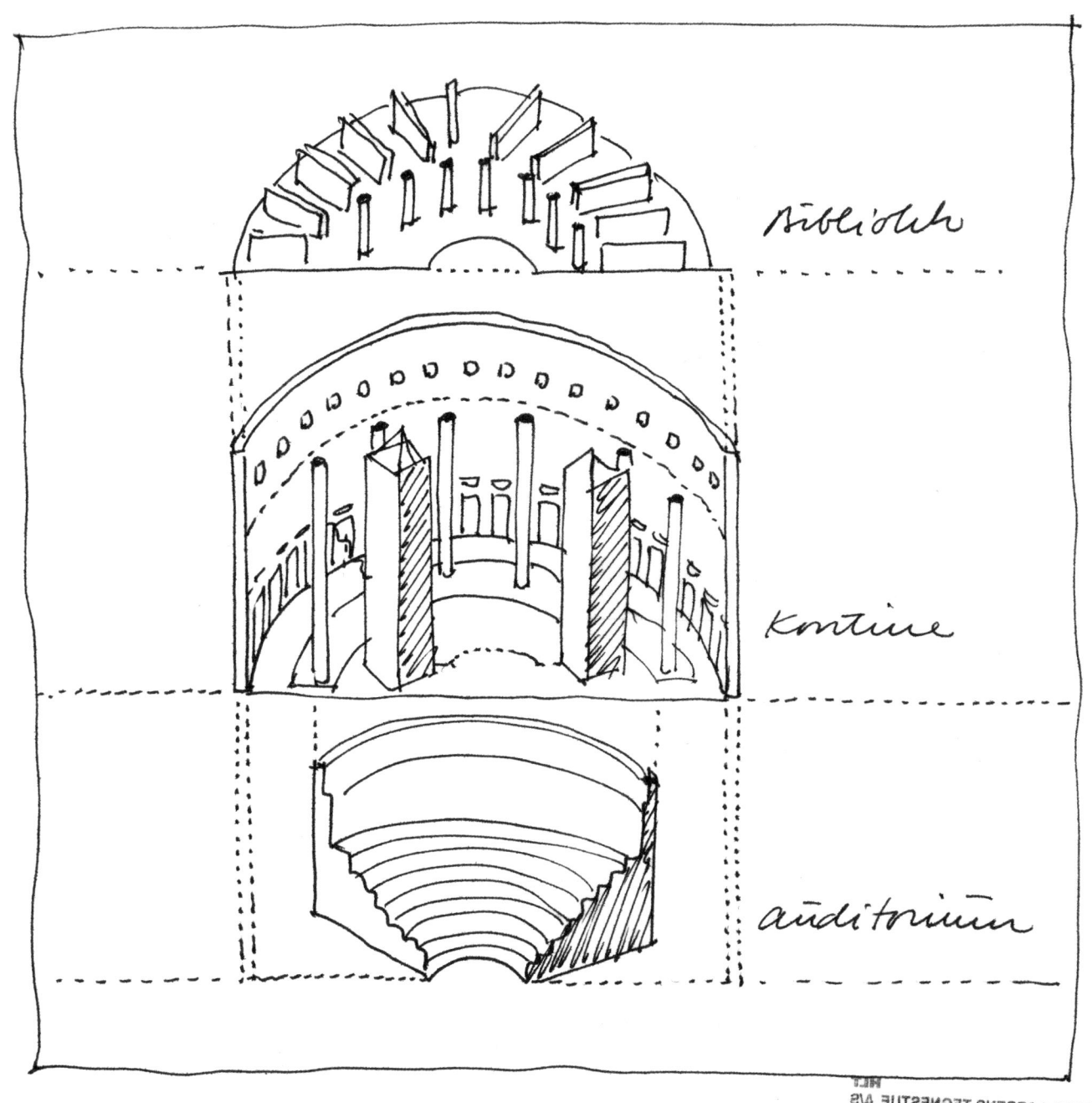

kantine

auditorium

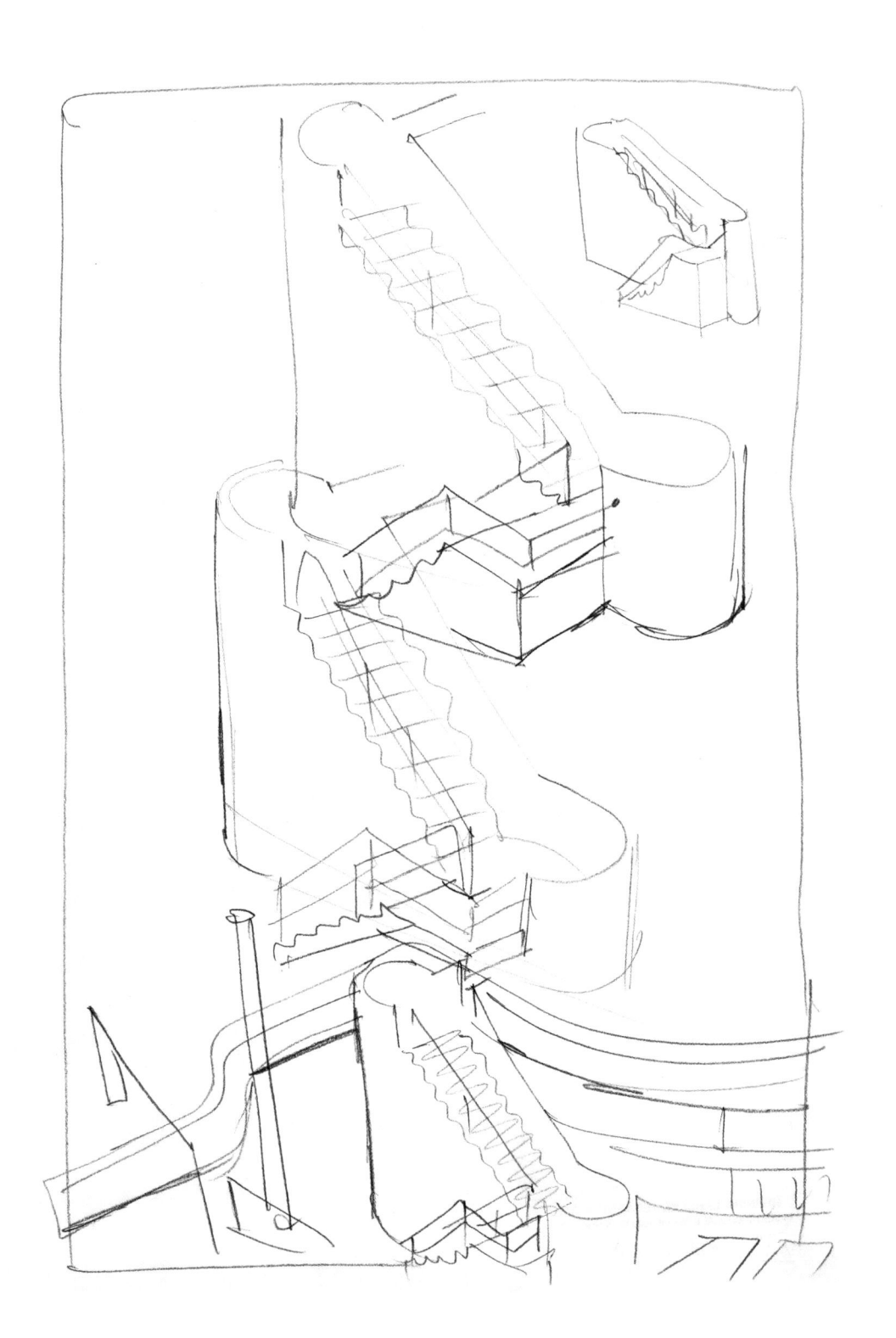

Copenhagen Business School
and Dalgas Have

141

Sketchbook from Malta

As the office grew bigger and there were more projects undertaken across the world, Henning Larsen's role in the office changed. He still went from table to table and discussed and drew projects with partners and associates, but there are not as many of these analytical and open-ended drawings left.

However, Larsen never stopped using drawing as a way of understanding the world. A small sketchbook from a holiday on Malta shows how he examined his experience through analytical drawing, not as a base for new projects but out of curiosity and the joy of experiencing his surroundings. The sketches study planning, urban spaces, buildings and even a painting by Caravaggio.

Sketchbook from Malta

15/9/91

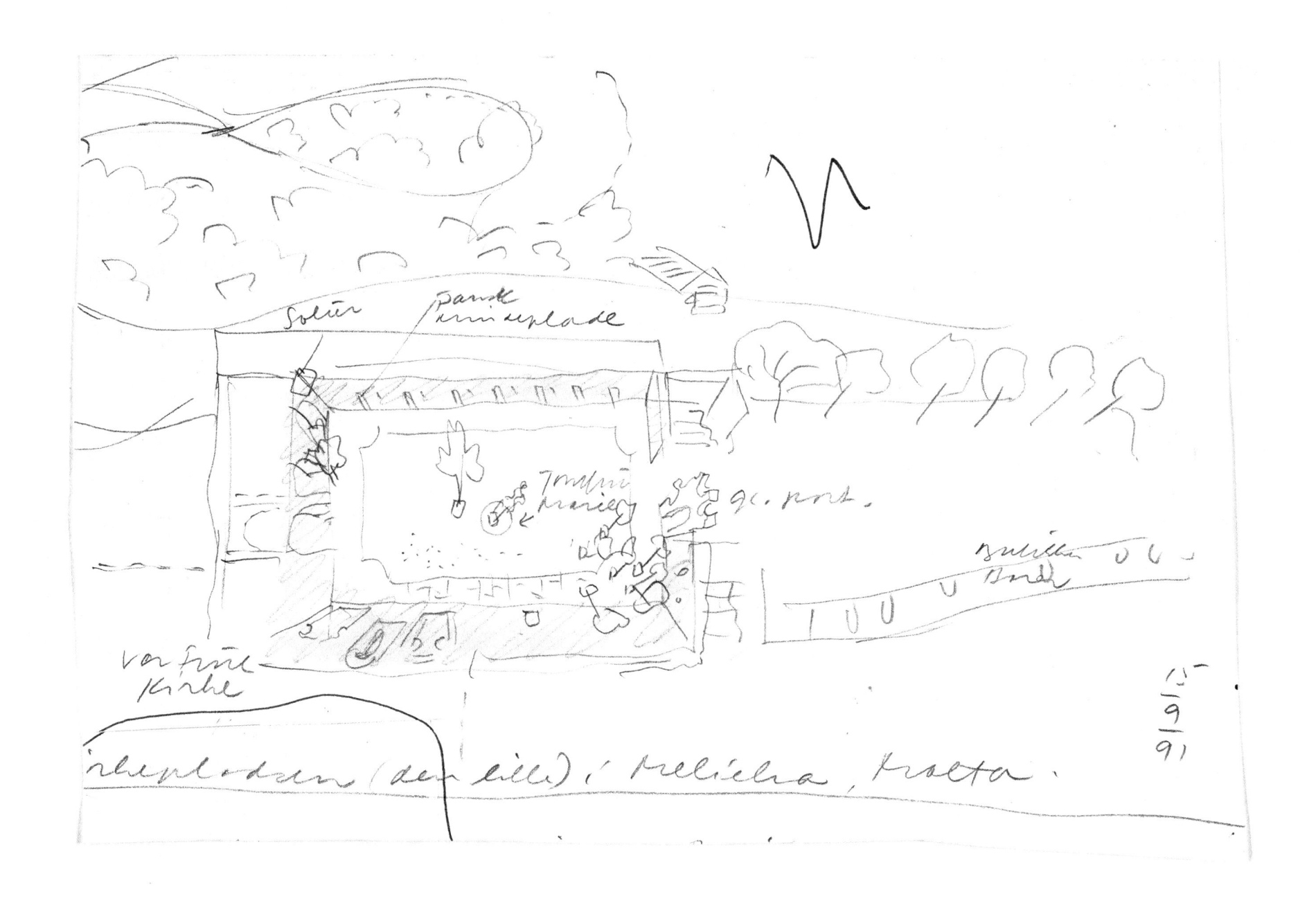

Sketchbook from Malta

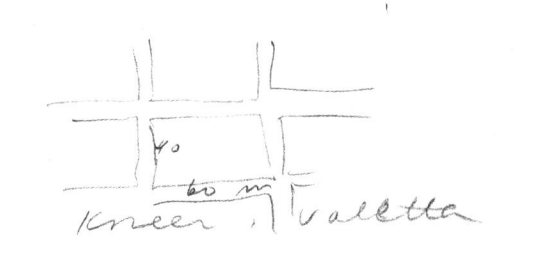

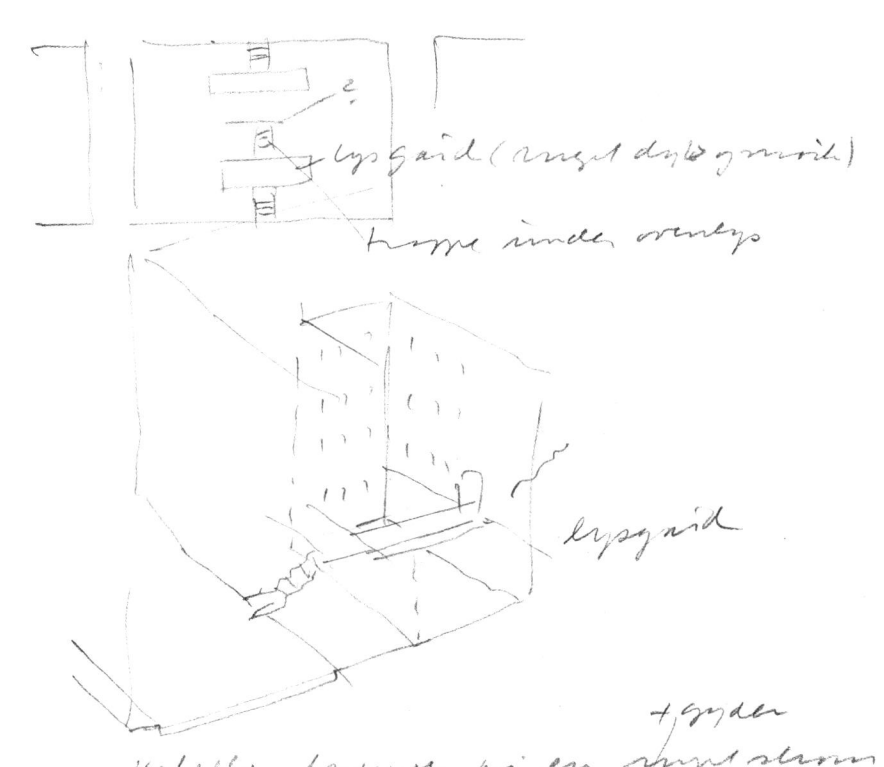

Kroer i Valletta

lysgård (meget dybt og smal)

trappe inde ovenlys

lysgård

+ gyder

Valletta bygget på en rigid stram renæssance-gadenet-system, med trædere i smalere gader. Alle blotte gyder hvor kroen ud - (ingen forhave er tilladt) - kun små gyder inde i massivet - indeliden et indre glasoverdækket rum

Sketchbook from Malta

15/9/91

Manoel Teatret

ligger i en af de mindre side-gaden (Theatre street) og er et forfinet hus i 3 etager men en beskeden indgang

Forhal og Foyer var under re-parationer – der var indret-tet en drama skole i mezza-ninen. Der stod et meget smukt grand piano i brunt træ (mørk) meget elegant og flot og enkelt. Teatret er lille – scenen godt 6 m bred – orkestergraven til 30 – 270 på gulvet og alt i alt ca 600 tilskuere – gulv + 4 balko-ner – den øverste for stående.

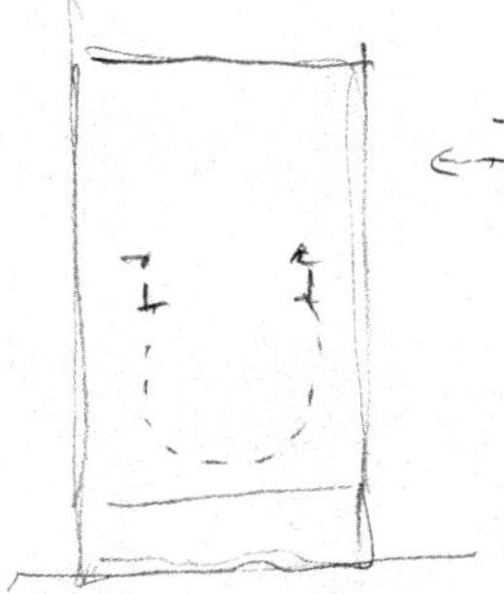

153

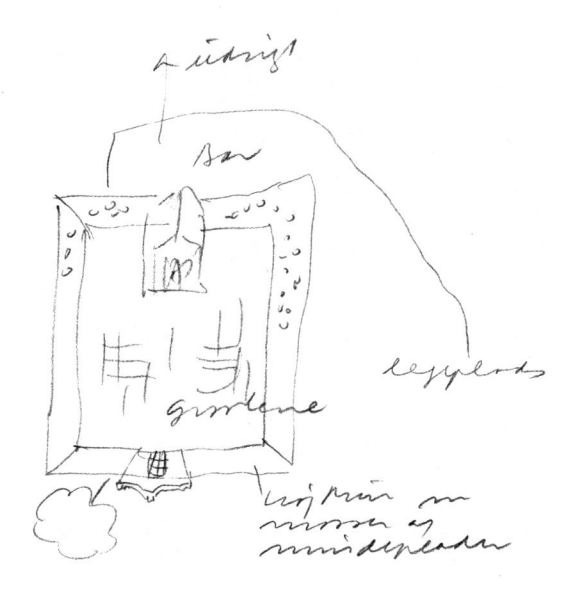

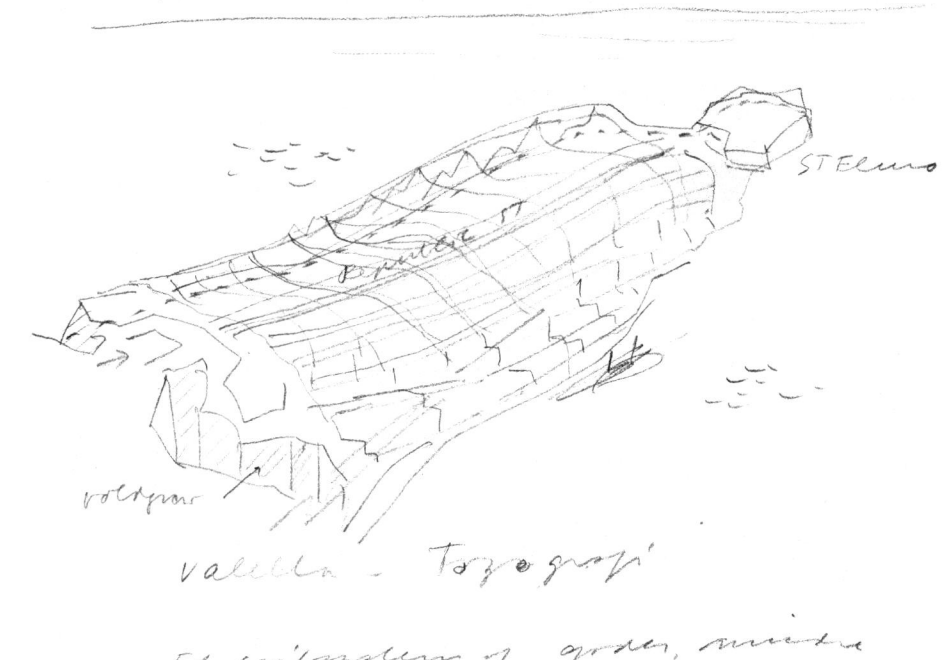

Bibliography

Abel, Chris: "Ministry of Foreign Affairs, Riyadh". *Architectural Review*, 1985/1061, pp.24-39

Barizza, Elisabetta and Marco Falsetti (ed.): *Rome and the Legacy of Louis I. Kahn.* Routledge, 2018

"Den nordiske konkurrence om hospital i Hvidovre". *Arkitekten*, 1963/18, pp. 333-348

"Konkurrencen om et Industriens Hus og en bygning for Aktieselskabet De Forenede Bryggerier". *Arkitekten*, 1965/15, pp. 293-313

Korn, Arthur: *Glas im Bau und als Gebrauchsgegenstand.* Ernst Pollak Verlag, 1929

Korn, Arthur: *History builds the Town.* Lund Humphries, 1953

Larsen, Henning: "Mor Danmark". *A+B (Arkitektur og Billedkunst)*, 1970/1-4

Le Corbusier: *Vers une Architecture.* Éditions Crès, 1924

Lund, Nils-Ole: *Arkitekt Henning Larsen.* Gyldendal, 1996

Lund, Nils-Ole and Kim Dirckinck-Holmfeld: "Handelshøjskolen på Frederiksberg. Den kgl. danske ambassade i Riyadh, Saudi Arabien. Administrationsbygning for Færch Plast, Holstebro. Diverse arbejder af Henning Larsen". *Arkitektur DK*, 1989/2, pp. 49-104

Millech, Knud and Kay Fisker (ed.): *Danske Arkitekturstrømninger 1850-1950: En arkitekturhistorisk undersøgelse.* Østifternes Kreditforening, 1951

"Ministry of Foreign Affairs, Riyadh, Saudi Arabia: The Aga Khan Award for Architecture 1989". *Architectural Review*, 1989/1113, pp. 96-98

Møller, Henrik Sten: *Legen og lyset. En frise over Henning Larsen som menneske og arkitekt.* Politiken, 2000

Nygaard, Axel: *Tegninger.* København, 1943

Sarvig, Ole: *Palle Nielsen.* Carit Andersen, 1966

Sharp, Dennis (ed.): *Planning and Architecture: Essays presented to Arthur Korn by the Architectural Association.* Barrie and Rockliff, 1967

Skovgaard Lassen, K.J. and Claus M. Smidt: *Tegning. Danske arkitekters tegninger fra det 20. århundrede.* Aschehoug, 2006

Skriver, Poul Erik: "Freie Universität Berlin: 2. præmie projekt". *Arkitekten*, 1964/14, pp. 292-293

Skriver, Poul Erik: "PH-konkurrencen". *Arkitekten*, 1965/2, pp. 21-37

Skriver, Poul Erik and Kim Dirckinck-Holmfeld: "Arbejder af Henning Larsen". *Arkitektur DK*, 1980/4, pp. 129-172

Smidt, Claus M.: "Fra Tempel til boligblok", i *Kunstakademiet 1754-2004*, bd. 1, p. 321. Det Kongelige Akademi for de Skønne Kunster og Arkitektens Forlag, 2004

Venice Biennale: *Architecture, 1980: The presence of the past.* Rizzoli, 1980

**The Architectural Sketches
of Henning Larsen**

© 2022 Merete Ahnfeldt-Mollerup
and Strandberg Publishing

Editor: Louise Haslund-Christensen
Assistent editor: Anna Sarelin
Copy editor: Wendy Brouwer
Graphic design: Rasmus Koch Studio
The book is set in: AG Book Pro
Paper: Tauro Offset 150 g
Image processing: Narayana Press, Gylling
Printing and binding: Printer Trento, Italy

Printed in Italy, 2022
1. edition, 1. printrun
ISBN: 978-87-94102-93-3

With the exception of the below mentioned the
illustrations in the book come from Royal Danish Library
– Danish National Art Library.
Lone Backe's Archive: 17-18, 20L, 81, 86, 88-90, 105-109, 142-151
Arkitekten: nr. 25 1965: 59

Copying from this book is only permitted at institutions
that have made agreements with Copydan,
and only within the framework of these agreements.

Strandberg Publishing A/S
Gammel Mønt 14
DK-1117 Copenhagen K
www.strandbergpublishing.dk